Join Me In The Garden

"Grow Your Own And Taste The Difference"

By George Walters

Also by George Walters...

~~~

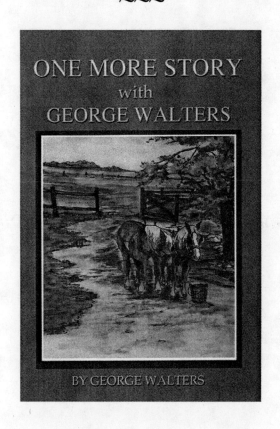

& Coming Soon

~~~

Moments In Time
Available In The Spring Of 2010

Acclaims

for

My First Book
"One More Story with George Walters"

"George Walters is more than a storyteller, he's a keeper of the past. Our world has changed so much in one lifetime. From gramophone to ipod, from horsepower to solar energy, this world has become a place of speed, convenience and superpowers. With all the advances, much has been lost. In an era where text and imagery can be electronically filed in countless volumes, memory is the unique storehouse that links us to our ancestors, our evolution as a species, our fundamental attachment to this earth.

George Walters' gentle and insightful recollections take us back to our roots. He brings color to the black and white photographs of an era that is rapidly dissolving into a romanticized "video" to those of us who've never ploughed a field or taken water from a well.

With honesty, humor and sweet colloquial speech, he draws you into his private life, generously sharing his thoughts, his recollections and his caring philosophy. His short stories are Canadian history at its' best. Read them and pass them on to the next generation, for this is what and who we are. These stories are part of our inheritance, with grateful thanks to people like George Walters; our keepers of the past."

Lynn Johnston, Creator of For Better or For Worse
Corbeil, Ontario

Here Are A Few More Kind Words From My Extended Family Of Readers

Times change and technology changes. But telling a good story never does. And George Walters is a shining example of what a good story can do to a reader.

George has been entertaining Nugget readers for years with his tales that harken back to a forgone era, a simpler time - all through the magic of his words.

Steve Hardy
Managing Editor
North Bay Nugget
North Bay, Ontario

****

George Walters tells engaging stories and in the process takes us back to a simpler time, even if those times for most of us, exist only in our imagination. He is by the way of being a sort of bucolic philosopher with many of his anecdotes illustrating eternal truths or expounding life lessons in a straightforward and interesting way.

Pete Handley, North Bay, Ontario
TVCogeco, "Life Is"

****

George Walters has a gentle humour, and a deep sense of what is most important about living every day fully with love and respect for people and nature. His home-spun voice is authentic and charming. His stories are peopled by animals and humans that you would love to spend time with, (except, of course, the most ornery ones.) The illustrations bring even more fun and charm to the stories.

Suzanne Brooks
Gulliver's Quality Books and Toys
North Bay, Ontario

****

I would recommend George's books to anyone that enjoys reminiscing about quieter times. I have read and given away many of George's books to relatives and friends because I know they will read and enjoy a book like this. I am looking forward to reading the next book from George.

Ian Buckham
Beatty Printing, North Bay, Ontario

iv

****

Congratulations on the success of your first book, "One More Story." It has brought back warm memories of our early years and life in a rural community.

Good Luck on the launch of your new book. Hartley is an avid gardener and we will look forward to reading your newest endeavor, and perhaps learning some tips from your vast experiences.

Hartley & Sherry Moore
White Birches Camp, Loring, Ontario

****

How lucky we are to have George and Ruth Walters move to Port Loring and become a part of our community. Many of us are losing the knowledge of living off of the land and we benefit from George sharing his knowledge with us through his articles in the paper and in his book, "One More Story."

We are very much looking forward to reading his next book.

Kerry & Marla Booth
Port Loring, Ontario

****

It is nice to see a couple that is so community minded, and treats this place as though it has always been their home, even though they have only been here a short while. I have enjoyed and appreciated George's stories and practical advice every time he stops in.

Mike Clapperton
Loring, Ontario

****

Like a visit with your friendly neighbor, the time spent reading, "One More Story with George Walters," bring wit, wisdom and a touch of humor into your day. You'll be happy you, "popped in."

Dr. Graham Wood
Commanda, Ontario

****

Reading his written word is like having George right in the room. It is an entertaining and heart warming read for all ages. The book makes you yearn for a simpler life.

Jeannine & Phil Welton
Northern Lights Resort, Loring, Ontario

****

"George Walters' book has been a trip back in time for many. Readers responses have been appreciation at a chance to revisit years gone by. George recounts events during his maturing years as a young lad in rural Ontario. Common sense solutions to problems, interacting with level-headed folk, appreciation of nature and a genuine love of life radiate throughout the pages of the book.

The book is the author's genuine willingness to share past experiences with the reader. An easy-to-read volume well written in everyday language anyone can easily follow, the reader is treated to a good visit with a long-time country friend.

Ruth Walters excellent pen and ink illustrations for each chapter enhance the book well. Each picture entices the reader to locate the picture somewhere in pages of the individual chapter.

The book has been a completely family-produced volume including writing, illustrating, editing, proofreading and promoting of sales.

George's recollection of rural life entice the reader to ask, "When is the next volume going to be ready to read?"

Good luck to George, Ruth and family in their future endeavors.

Meanwhile put me on the growing list willing to purchase future volumes on any topic."

I'm looking forward to the next volume. Keep on writing!

Lois Sinclair, Marten River
Columnist, Community Voices

****

I have never read such an interesting down to earth book, I felt like I was right there with him, so real and so true, couldn't put it down, and I am not a real reader. I'm sure the second book will be just as great, thanks George.

Marylou Francoeur
St. Thomas, Ontario

****

If you haven't read George's stories before, your in for a treat. George is my long time friend and buddy. He is all about being, down home on the Canadian farm, but we all can relate.

This is a family affair, George writes and his wife Ruth does the art work, and his two boys are the tech support. Great job folks.

Frank Cianciolo
Chelsea, Michigan, U.S.A.

****

George Walters has storytelling down to a fine art. A comfortable read. Relax and enjoy tales of a simple way of life, filled with caring and sharing. Ruth Walters beautifully illustrates each story.

Congratulations on a fine book, I look forward to more.

Bonnie Gorham
Loring General Store, Loring, Ontario

****

Fascinating and light-hearted accounts of life in Rural communities that bring back fond memories of years gone by, with amazing artistry that make the stories come to life.

A refreshing and entertaining reading journey that mixes country tradition with ever changing modern life.

We look forward to more great stories and many more books.

Kevin, Betty and Staff
Powassan Farm & Pet Centre- Country Depot
South River Lumber- Farm & Pet Centre

****

Captivating, nostalgic stories which will entertain the country kid in all- well illustrated.

Gary&Pat Robinson
Michigan, U.S.A.

****

Reading George Walters book is like taking a journey with him, meeting all his closest old friends....the kindness of a simpler time is refreshing.

Judy Whitmell
Port Loring, Ontario

Join Me
In The Garden

By George Walters

Published 2009

ISBN: 978-0-9809884-1-3

Join Me
In The Garden

George Walters
Illustrations by Ruth Walters

Ruth Walters being a self taught artist has been bringing stories to life through her work for over 40 some years. This second book of her husbands is just another example of how she is able to capture a piece of time and bring out in vivid detail the true meaning of each story. Her sketches through out the book is done in such a leisurely and reflective way, that it keeps the reader yearning for more.

Seldom does all these qualities meet within one woman. Such a woman is Ruth.

Acknowledgments

My deepest thanks goes out to all those that have helped with this book in one way or another. My wife Ruth, my two sons, Craig & Karl, all the folks in & around my home town of Port Loring, Newspapers, Magazines, Book Stores and all the Small Business's that have helped in the promotion of my first book. Not to forget all my extended family of readers that have taken the time to; Call, Visit, E-mail & Write me.

And finally: Over the years I have found that some folks liked my advice so much that they have framed it and hung it on the wall. That's fine and dandy, but there comes a time that just looking at something doesn't get the job done.

This Book Is Dedicated To

My Wife Ruth & My Two Sons
Craig & Karl
and
In Memory Of
Reg, Laura, Grey Wolf & My Dad Earl

Table of Contents

Table Of Contents

Table Of Contents

Preface

Who is George Walters? Well, during a TV Interview of his first
book, the host of the show asked if he thought of himself as a Country
Philosopher. Giving this some thought he decided on looking up the word
Philosopher in the dictionary, and low and behold he found that is exactly
what he is.

Literally a lover of wisdom, sometimes also called a seeker of truth. Not
just any truth, but truth about important basic, elusive issues, such as what is
right and wrong, what is sure, what is human? These are the questions he
confronts when everyday thinking is inadequate.

He has devoted over 60 years to the search. But this is only part of the
story. He pursues truth regardless of popularity, fashion or legislation. He
needs to have clear thinking and reasoning to be able to juggle complex
information, and be able to break it down to plain English, as much as
possible. He spends much time carefully weeding out all the falsehoods and
contradictions, and putting down on paper his and other folks experiences to
help the people he cares most about, and to make this a better country for
them to grow up in.

George has been writing and sharing his wisdom in Newspapers,
Magazines and through Public Speaking for many years. His extended
family of readers have come to know and love him through his easy down to
earth way he portrays his message. His captivating ways of writing
heightens the readers awareness as his stories unfold in front of them, giving
them the strength and comfort like a life long friend, lending a helping hand.

Preface

George has learned a lot growing up on the farm, including the simple easy ways of the old time gardeners. The little tricks and tips he has learned from these old timers are shared with you, as well as information about health, plant recognition, and recipes too.

He is a Story-Teller with the ability to take you back through time to an era where folks knew how to fend for themselves, a place where folks grew their own crops, survived the harsh elements that Mother Nature threw at them, and most importantly, a place where families were one.

It's a book for all ages and is a must for anyone with even a passing interest for country living, wanting to plant a garden, or those that just want to take in what Mother Nature has to offer.

So find your favorite chair, sit back, and if you find this book doesn't give you the urge to get out there and do some plantin', you had better read it again. Enjoy!

Join Me
In The Garden

By George Walters

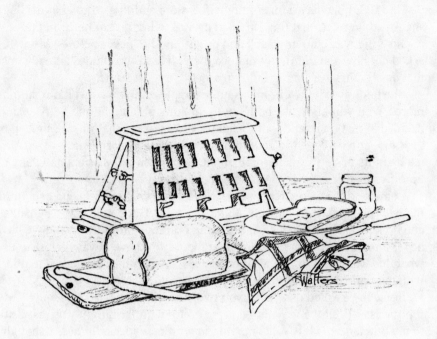

Country Living

Y ou know for most folks every day life consists of getting out of bed, doing their chores around the house and going to work for the rest of the day. Now for my wife and I, well ours is similar, but we choose to work for ourselves and not others. Our day begins with getting out of bed, having a tea or two, then enjoying a nice breakfast. My wife keeps telling me that breakfast is the main meal of the day, which is so true. I have found with a full stomach I can pretty well tackle anything that happens throughout the day, mentally or physically.

While we are having breakfast we like to thrash over life in itself and while chatting enjoy a game of crib or two. Once done, I am off to the wood-working shop making things for our store, in the garden, or if the urge is there, I sit down to writing a story or two. My wife usually does her work around the house, then she is off to her studio or outside helping me.

Some folks say it sure must be nice, I say, it's up to what one really wants in life. What we have today sure didn't come easy, it took a lot of hard work, mistakes, you name it, but here we are now and things couldn't be better, in spite of the way the old world is going. We didn't have anything given to us through life, like money, land or what ever, we earned every cent and then some.

Had a Gal one day come to my wife's store and they got to talking. What she found out was, that this lady had moved to her dream home in the country and was enjoying each and every day like never before. My wife asked her how she did it, not that we didn't live in the country already, just that our country was being built up around us at the time.

She told my wife, well, it was quite simple really, we just did it, nothing more. Well you know we both got to thinking about that bit of advice and decided to just do it, and that's what we did. We put the for sale sign up on the farm, and here we are now living in Northern Ontario, surrounded by nature at its best. Come to think about it, it's been a few years now, boy does time fly.

Some said we were crazy, some asked how we could give up everything that we had worked so hard for all those years. But you know, when all said and done, we both feel that we made the best move of our life and we have never looked back with doubt. Throughout life I have always felt that it's not what one wants in life, it's what one needs. We both have worked that in with our daily activities and it has done us well.

Some have asked us. "I bet you two sure miss the farm life, huh?" My reply was. "Well the way things were going with farming it was just getting to my wife and I. New folks moving in with new ideas. I guess I shouldn't resent them I suppose, but I do. No doubt they bring prosperity to some but they've changed things as I knew them for so long. I liked the country better as it was. Seemed we worked to set things up the way we liked them, then something moves in to scramble the picture. All life is change and readjustment I suppose."

But here where we live now it's like stepping back in time. I know it also will change some in the coming years, but for now we will enjoy each day as it is brought to us.

I gotta' say we have been doing that too, as I have been working with a couple old apple trees that were on the place when we bought it, trying to bring them back to a productive state. Raspberries have been planted, new gardens being established, well you name it. Guess that old saying, that you can take the boy out of the country but you can't take the country out of the boy is sure true. We live more in the country now than we ever did, here in Northern Ontario, but at a much smaller scale.

And remember this, anyone can have what we have today, just that they might have to give up a wee bit, to make their dreams come true.

Not Just A Pond

Our farm years ago was spread out over about a hundred acres and along one side of it, there was a kind of valley with a creek running through it. Well, with growing a lot of tender fruit and fresh vegetables, my old Dad decided that he would put up a dam at one end of the valley. Reason being that if we happen onto a real dry year, we would have enough water for irrigation.

Thinking back on how it all started, Dad had made friends with a feller that had a good size dozer. One night he called him up and got to tellin' him about his plan. The following day the fellow dropped by, they went over things again and the day after that, he was there with his equipment ready for work. After two coffees and a couple of home made muffins, off they went, with us young ones trailin' behind. This was real exciting stuff for us young fellers, as we didn't get to see big equipment too often, at least not close up and working.

Well he cleared off the bottom of the valley where the pond would be and pushed all the debris up to one end, which would become the dam. In the middle of the dam, Dad put in an over flow pipe and at the one end a run off, or what some call an over-flow, just in case we had a big storm. We sure didn't need the dam washing out after all the hard work in making it.

It sure was something to see when all said and done as there was over an acre of water, amazing too just how fast the pond filled up. What used to be a whole lot of nothing, was now filled with clear cold water.

3

It sure made my old Dad happy, as now no matter how dry the summers became, he would always have lots of water readily available for his vegetables and things.

The pond also made us young ones happy, as now we had a place to go swimming on them hot summer days and a place to skate on them winter days.

I got to thinking one day and went and asked my Dad about fish and was wondering if we could stock it. I told him I had heard a fellow talking about stocking his pond, the last time we were down at the hardware store. Dad didn't say too much but he did say he would look into it when he got some time, which he did.

A few weeks later a fellow dropped by, from the Lands And Forest Office and I listened while he was talking with my Dad.

"First thing," he said, "you need a pond big enough and it must have fresh cold water running in and out of it at all times if you want to stock it with trout, bass or both."

"Well," said Dad, "lets go for a walk."

I kind of thought by looking at the fellow and the way he was talking, that he thought it was just a waste of his time, but once he seen how big the pond was, he just said, "Wow!"

"Is that big enough," Dad asked?

"Sure is," he said and with that he went to look things over.

The water that ran into the pond came from the escarpment that our property backed up to and Dad told him that no matter how bad a summer got, the creek never dried up.

In a week or so, we had a truck loaded with fish, waiting at our door step.

"Where would you like them," the fellow asked?

"Follow me," Dad said and off we went down to the pond.

At that time they had a program to stock ponds free of charge, or large bodies of fresh water. Well, the fish were put in and a year later, I was out there with my pole. I gotta' tell ya, over the years we had many a good meal from that pond. I also had friends coming out of my ears on weekends wanting to go fishing. Dad finally had to stop a bit of it, as if we didn't, the pond would have been fished out.

Thinking back my old Dad did a lot of things like that, things that made life a lot easier. He made do with what was there and made money without spending it.

He used to tell me. "George, stay on top of things." Good sound advice, from a wise old man.

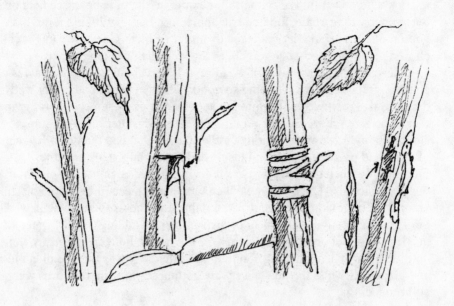

A Couple Ideas On Grafting

Moving here to the north I remember one spring I decided to see if I could bring back one of the old apple trees that was on our property, as it had gone wild with no one looking after it. A few days before though, my wife and I were out looking around at a nursery and spotted some Spy apple trees on sale. Looking at the price I decided that we should have one, so I bought it and planted it a few yards from the wild one.

An important tip is, you don't get many apples from just one tree. You need two at the very least for pollination. What I did though was take it one step further. I decided on taking a branch from the Spy that we just bought and graft it onto the wild tree. I gotta' say I have had pretty good luck with my grafting of trees over the years. I also have had pretty good luck in grafting different varieties of fruit all on one tree.

For example I remember one year back on the farm we had this one field with old pear trees on it. Well Dad and me got to thinking and we decided to see if we could take a Bartlett pear tree and graft some Bosc branches onto it. Worked great and eventually we had the whole field done up. Was quite a site for sure and had a lot of other farmers drop by for a look see.

George Walters

There is a lot of things folks can do like that and it doesn't mean one has to stick with just fruit trees either. For example, the old apple tree here on our property didn't have too good an apple on it being wild, but it did have a good root system, so why not take advantage of that. Guess you might call it cheating a bit on Mother Nature, but I am sure she doesn't mind.

One year I remember my Dad and myself had about twenty five acres of concord grapes that wasn't doing so good. They were old and pretty well dying back. Well we got to thinking about some of these new hybrid grapes that some farmers were bringing into our country. After giving it some careful thought, we went over to another farmer that had planted a few acres of them and picked up all the vines he had laying on the ground after pruning. We then got busy and grafted a piece of vine onto the bottom of all our old concords. Once done, we then wrapped a piece of bendable plastic around the bottom and sealed it. Doing that enabled us to keep the new grafts moist throughout the heat of the summer by adding a bit of water when needed. In about one month the most of them took hold and were growing on their own. The nice thing about doing it this way was that we didn't loose any grapes, as while the new ones were getting started, the concords were still producing.

Once the new hybrids got up to size and producing we then cut the concords off, leaving just the new vine. Didn't take long either, in two years we had our first crop which passed all our expectations. If we would have planted them from root it would have taken three years instead of two and cost us thousands of dollars.

A few years later we had folks come from Germany to see how we went about it. They took the information back to their country and it worked real well, so they said in a letter.

Another way of starting a new grapevine using the original vine, is to leave one extra long runner on the vine, with buds about six inches apart. Now take that runner that is still attached to the main stock and stretch it out on the ground putting a shovel full of soil over one section of it. Now bring the end back up to the wires and tie it. In one year you will be able to cut it from its mother and there you go, one free grape vine. Do that enough and you got yourself enough free vines to make your own home made wine for Christmas.

That's what I enjoy the most, the free part and the satisfaction of being different. In the long run it pays off, the vines or trees you do the grafting on, will be better than the ones you buy.

In saying that, now a days that's all they do, they just take a real hearty vine or tree, graft a new type onto it and that's what you get. The whole thing boils down to a good root system, so why not do it yourself.

Well there you have it, a bit of the old meets the new, with Mother Nature taking it from there.

A Bit On Tree Trimming

Most of my pruning was done when the trees were dormant, between the time when the leaves dropped in late fall, right up till the buds began to swell in early spring. The safest and best time I have found is just before the buds swell. The most risky time is very late fall and early winter.

I have found that dormant pruning of peach and nectarine increases the risk of winter injury and I prefer not to prune them until the flower buds have advanced sufficiently, this way I can see how the trees have weathered the winter.

A few years back I got to trimming one of my old apple trees we have here on the property. We have a few but this one really got out of hand. Anyways, looking at it I decided to see if I could bring it back to where it would have a few apples, instead of just growing branches.

The first pruning I cut about three feet off the top, then thinning the branches throughout the rest of the tree. Didn't take too much care, as at that time I just wanted to get it down a bit so I could handle it easier. The following year I took it a step further and got into trimming it properly.

The first thing one has to do is to stand back and take a good look at the tree. Up the center there is a main stock. Once in awhile though, you might come up against a tree that has more than one main stock. If that should happen, pick the straightest one making sure that there is sufficient branches

7

striking off from it. Once you are sure you got the nicest one, cut the other one off.

Next you look for any branches that are crossing over onto others and cut them off, as you don't need them rubbing together.

Then look for the real nice looking buds that are close together, they are what you want to keep as they will be what gives you some fruit.

At the end of each branch every year, about a foot long or so, will be new growth, this can be cut off, unless you need or want a new branch to fill in somewhere. For most parts they are just cut off leaving the larger buds at the bottom.

Once you have this all done, look up at the top, you will probably see a good amount of shoots sticking straight up. These are all new growth and don't produce anything. What I do with mine, I cut them off to where I can easily reach them with a step ladder. You might have to cut into the good branches a wee bit to get the tree down to size if it is over grown, like I had to do, but it has to be done.

Once you got this all finished, step back and look at the tree again. It should be a lot more open looking with no branches touching or crossing over each other. I like to keep my branches going in a vertical direction.

I would also like to mention here about your pruners. When buying a pair of pruners you will need a long handle one and a hand held one. Buy a good pair as you will have and need them for years. Best place to buy, is go to a good nursery, hardware store or farm dealership and see what they have.

Mine were made in Germany and I have had them for years. Must have trimmed thousands of trees and grape vines with them and they still work like a charm. Also pick up a small hand file suited for the job, as you will want to keep them sharp, it is important that you have a nice clean cut to ward off disease. Always remember, when you cut a branch or vine, keep the flat side of the pruners to the tree, so when you cut the branch it makes a smooth cut with no nubs. Through my eyes there is nothing worse than to see a tree with a whole bunch of stubs sticking out, or so to speak.

If your tree hasn't been trimmed in a long time and is quite large don't rush into it, make it a fun project. Don't worry too much about making a mistake here and there, as for most parts the tree is forgiving. Then once all done, stand back and have a look at it, you will just know in your mind what it should look like, I guarantee it.

Bottom line is this; make sure you don't cut off the old buds that are close together.

Remove any branches that are crossing or rubbing up against each other.

Find a main stock and train it by removing others.

Cut off all suckers or new growth at the end of each branch. You can tell this by the lighter color, along with that the suckers and new growth won't have any buds to speak of.

And finally, thin out the center of the tree so there can be lots of air movement.

With these things all done up, you should be on your way to becoming a master tree trimmer. I got faith in you and what can be better than to get out into the fresh air, take an old tree and bring it into something that will give you years of delicious fruit.

Also don't forget to water your fruit trees and things if you happen on a real dry year. I put together a chart for you to make things a bit easier.

Watering Chart

Apple	Low-Medium,	Water during long dry spells.
Apricot	Medium,	Infrequent, deep watering.
Blackberry	High,	Water during growing season.
Blueberry	Very High,	Frequent water.
Cherry	High,	Regular, deep watering.
Red Currant	High,	Regular water.
Gooseberry	High,	Water to maintain growth.
Grape	Low-Medium,	Little water once established.
Nectarine	High,	Water while fruit is forming in hot weather.
Peach	High,	Water while fruit is forming in hot weather.
Pear	Medium-High,	Regular water during growing season.
Plum	Medium,	Best with some deep watering in summer.
Raspberry	High,	Regular water.
Strawberry	Very High,	Frequent, deep soaking.

So there you have it, a bit on trimming, and remember this, don't make it complicated as it isn't, enjoy yourself.

Gossip

Gossip, now there is a juicy topic for some folks. I know some think it doesn't have too much of a place in todays world, but if one takes a close look at it, one will find it's just a word, and, well, words can't hurt ya, or can they?

I have found that it's only human nature for men or women to spread some news that was given to them, it gives them a feeling of recognition. I have done it, sometimes not even knowing I did. Over the years I have found no human being can be trusted, when it comes to spreading gossip.

I have also found that if one doesn't like to hear their name being brought up by folks when they walk by others, then they should try and keep their private business to themselves.

Living in a small town gossip tends to be more pronounced I have found, but that is because everybody knows everybody and it's pretty hard not to hear something about someone when going to the store, or just out for a walk.

Now on the other hand, there is good things about gossip, yep, good things.

For example, years ago back on the farm there wasn't too many houses that were close to us, but we did have friends. We also had a meeting place in a near-by town and on any given Sunday, that's where folks met. Back then it wasn't a place to praise one special person, it was a place to share ideas, help others and get on with living a good way of life. Laura always said, "the best sermons are lived, not preached." Wished there was more of that today, but times have changed.

At the meeting place, Reg, Laura and myself found out a bit of gossip now and then about new folks that moved to town, which in some cases was a good thing. Reason being, if they were in need, it was a way of folks to come to their aid. It didn't happen that often though as back then most folks were too proud to ask for help. In some instances that is a good way to be, in some not so good, especially if there happens to be young ones running around in need.

On one visit we found a new family that moved in to an old farm house with two young ones, girl and boy around the age of seven or so, about my age at that time. At the meeting place we found that they didn't have enough food to hold them over through the winter. Just happened the young girl at the meeting place was seen by me putting food in her pockets. I didn't say anything at the time, as I figured if she was hungry, let her take what she wanted, as that is what the food was there for.

Later on at home I got to telling Reg and Laura about what I had seen and they put together some potatoes, corn and things and we took a ride over to their place. We had to make it look diplomatic, as we didn't want them to think we were feeling sorry for them, which we weren't, we were just concerned. Ended up we made some real good friends.

Thing was back then that sometimes a fellow or gal might seem to be down and out, but in reality they have more to offer a town than some folks with everything. As we found out, this fellow was good at Black Smithing and in a year or so he opened up a spot in his old barn to shoe horses and do all kinds of things.

Also one shouldn't think that just because a person is dressed nicely that they couldn't be hurting, as I have found that to be the case a good many times.

A saying that I use quite a bit goes something like this. "To know how country folks are doing, look at their barns, not their houses."

Yep most of the old meeting halls have been closed up or torn down today and I got to say it sorrows me to know they are all but gone. If asked what I thought of Gossip in todays world? I would have to say this.

"It has its place."

Fresh Air

Y ou know every now and again, I get to thinking of how lucky us folks up here in the north are. For one, just think of the water you drink, especially if you have a good well. Our water here, where we live is excellent, other than a wee bit high in iron. But that's OK, as the old body needs a wee bit more iron as it gets older, or at least mine does.

Throughout the summer when I go to the tap it's hard not to notice how cold the water is, as one would have a hard time holding his hand under it. Can't beat that to combat the heat of summer, although we don't have too many hot days up here to deal with, which suites me just fine.

Some other benefits from the cold fresh well water, is all the minerals and things that one gets with just one glass.

Another would be how I enjoy bringing in some fresh vegetables from the garden, cutting them to size and letting them sit in the water for a few minutes before making a salad. I gotta' say it sure makes the veggies nice and crisp.

I did have a we bit of a problem with our tea making using the water from the well when we first moved here, as when the tea was introduced to the boiling water, we developed a scum on the top after it set in ones cup for a bit. I did a bit of thinking on the subject and remembered years ago Laura the lady of the house would take a teaspoon of fresh lemon juice and mix it with each pot and that got me to thinking. So I tried it and just about eliminated it, only thing is I don't really like the taste of lemon, just my luck huh?

On another note, when winter is upon us my wife and I start to open up a few jars of our preserves that we did up throughout the summer months. Pickled beets is one of my favorites and usually it is first on the list. We also get into a few of our fruits like strawberries, cherries, blueberries, peaches and rhubarb. We like to break up our meals a bit and each day have something different, as it makes for a health body. Nothing beats home grown vegetables and fruits come winter, not to forget the money one saves from not having to buy them in the store or drive to the store for that matter.

We have two freezers in the basement, not big ones but they are all we need. With the two small ones we can put our vegetables, fruits and things in one and all the other things like home made pies, meats in the other. This way it makes it easier for us to find things when needed. I should also mention here that the two small ones, I have found, doesn't cost as much as a big one. Hard to believe but true.

We also got a cold room down stairs and this is very helpful when it comes to storing fresh vegetables like turnips, potatoes, squash, apples and things. In my mind every home should have one of these, especially if they grow their own.

One quick tip here, never put your onions in with the rest of the vegetables. I always hang mine up on a nail in the main part of the basement preferably where its dry, away from my cold room. Reason being, onions and other vegetables, especially potatoes, don't store well together.

Another real benefit of living up here in the north is the fresh air. You know, since moving here my old nose has been sniffing out all kinds of things. I like to think the reason behind it is that with the fresh air and good eating, well, ones body is doing what it's suppose to be doing. Nothing like getting out of bed each morning, going outside and taking that first good breath of fresh air, I gotta' tell ya, it sure...... makes a fellow feel good to be alive.

One time coming back from town, my wife and I were mentioning to each other about how we could smell the cedars, pines, leaves and things, seemed as if they were jumping right out at us. On another trip to our sons, Craig and Karl, we were passing a dairy farm. My wife looked over at me and said.

"You know George, not all fresh country air smells as nice as you would like folks to believe."

Hmm, well, I just told her it was, roast beef on the hoof.

Plantain To The Rescue

There is all kinds of medicine out there in todays world, some for the good, some not so good and some just plain no good.

Thinking back to my younger days on the farm living with Reg and Laura, there wasn't many a spring that went by that we didn't have to deal with them pesky skeeter's and black flies. I would have to say though that the black flies were the worst. I kind of figured they were just down right mean, greedy one might say, as they take the whole piece and come back for more.

With that in mind each and every spring Laura and I would head on back to the fields to search out the broad leaf plant which was called, Common Plantain. It is pretty well found all across Ontario, most of Canada, along with parts of the United States.

The thing about plantain, it is good for all kinds of bites, cuts, bruises and even helps a bit with the arthritis. Now one would ask if it is safe to use? Well I can say this, over the years Laura used the leaves in the early spring for salads, so that should tell you something.

The way we used it if we needed a quick fix while working in the fields, would be to take one leaf and roll it between two fingers till you got the juice running. Then just take the juice and rub it on the insect bite. Works slick and you will find that the itch will be gone within minutes.

Another way of using this plant is, well lets say if you have a cut on your finger. If that happens just take a leaf and chew it, yep chew it, what that does it mixes with the saliva in your mouth and becomes an excellent antiseptic. Once chewed you can then put it on a cut which will heal in a short time. One thing you should remember before you put the chewed piece on a cut, make sure the wound is clean. The reason for this is that the plantain will heal the wound right over anything that might happen to be in the cut, like dirt and you wouldn't want that.

So what I do is, if I am not close to any soap or water, I kind of wash the cut with the blood that is coming out of the wound, then go ahead and put on the plantain. I know it sounds like it will hurt like the dickens' using ones own blood for cleaning. In reality though you are already hurting and moving the blood around right after you get the cut doesn't hurt hardly at all. Price you pay is small, for big rewards sometimes.

Now when it comes to making salve one would think it would be a difficult procedure but it isn't, simple really. The way Laura would do it would be to pick about one pound of leaves, roots, and seeds from the plant. In other words every part of it. She then takes them into the house, washes them real good in the sink and lets them dry on a tea towel.

While they are drying she then takes about one pound of pure lard, warms it up till it's melted, being careful not to let it boil. She then crushes up the plantain, leaves, roots and seeds and mix it with the lard. I use an old cast iron hand grinder, which I had given to me years ago, was used for grinding up vegetables, something like the old meat grinders. Works great too.

Once the plant pieces are added to the lard she would then set it back onto the old wood cook stove, get it boiling for one minute and then let it set for a half an hour on low heat. She then would take some cheese cloth and strain out the contents. After it was strained she would then put it in the ice fridge or the cold room for keeping. What you have now is pure plantain salve, which you can use for all kinds of problems that might arise throughout the summer and winter months.

After two or three months make a new batch and throw away the old. I make mine in early spring so we have some all summer and come fall I make some more for winter use. I also have found for longer storage one could do it up in small containers and freeze it.

I remember when I was young going to the old one room school house, with a small tin container full of the salve, which sat in my pocket just in case some nasty bug or a cut should arise throughout the day.

I should also mention here, if you are a bit worried that you might be allergic to the plant, then just take a wee bit of the leaf, squeeze some juice out of it and rub it on a small portion of your wrist, about the size of a dime. If it doesn't turn red your in business. I got to say in all my years I have never seen anyone that is allergic to the plant, but hey, you never know, better to take a wee bit of prevention just to make sure.

Well there you go, a bit on an old remedy which has fixed up my family and me more times than I can remember. So come this spring when those pesky skeeter's and black flies get to biting, you now have the fix.

You know, help is readily available using plants and things, but the problem is that today folks don't know where to look, what kinds are safe to use or what precautions one should take.

I have found though that a lot of old time fixes and things are still available. Where would I learn about such things one might ask? Well it's simple really, just seek out the Elders and ask questions, but don't wait too long, as every few minutes one of our old ones is taken from us.

Two simplified recipes for Plantain

1 - As tea for colds and flu use 1 tablespoon dry or fresh whole Plantain (seed, root, and leaves) to 1 cup boiling water, steep ten minutes, strain and sweeten to your liking. One cup in the morning and one cup after supper.

2 - To use as a healing salve: In a large non-metallic pan place 1lb. Of the entire Plantain plant, thoroughly washed and chopped, and 1 cup of lard, cover, cook down on low heat till all is mushy and green. Strain while hot, cool and use for burns, insect bites, rashes, sores and some say wrinkles. I haven't tried the last one myself, but........... might be a good idea.

Plantain also has other uses too

The leaves and the seed are medicinal used as an antibacterial, antidote, anti-inflammatory, antiseptic, laxative, poultice. Medical evidence also exists that says it can be uses as an alternative medicine for asthma, emphysema, bladder problems, bronchitis, fever, hypertension, rheumatism and blood-sugar control.

The roots are used in the treatment of a wide range of complaints including diarrhea, gastritis, peptic ulcers, irritable bowel syndrome, cystitis, bronchitis, catarrh, sinusitis, coughs, asthma and hay fever. It also causes a natural aversion to tobacco and is currently being used in stop smoking preparations.

Some say what if I take an allergic reaction to a plant? I say, did you ever read the possible side effects on some of the medicines of today, makes you think huh?

Bottom line is this. "Do the research, and use common sense."

Composting Made Easy

You know one item that every home owner should have is a composting box or composting area. I for one don't have anything special, other than a place that is out of the way where I can put things. The main thing about composting is putting in the right ingredients. Now in saying that don't think it's going to be complicated, as it isn't, actually composting is one of the easiest things one can do and one of the most rewarding too.

I use everything for mine other than some foods like meat or oils. I know some folks do, but here in the north one has to watch out for critters getting into it.

I like to start mine off with either leaves that has been chewed up with the mower, or some wood sawdust. On top of that I like to put some grass cuttings as they are loaded with nitrogen, which the composting process needs. The nitrogen is what gets the composting pile to cooking so to speak. If it isn't hot on the inside it isn't working.

As I said, for myself I have mine just put in a pile away from the house a bit, but you can build one real easy. If you only have a small garden you can probably get away with one about three feet by three feet, using plain rough cut, one inch by six inch boards.

An easy way to go about it, would be to cut four corner posts and nail the boards onto the posts, leaving the front open. Once your finished with the three sides, you can work it out so that you can install one board at a time on the open end, as the pile gets higher. Reason being it makes it easier to turn the compost as you gather it up.

Turning the compost is a very important step in the process. Each time you turn the pile it starts the process all over again and in no time you have some real nice black organic fertilizer for you gardens.

As I turn mine I just move the bottom stuff over a bit to one side and keep adding to the other. Pretty soon I have actually two piles, one new and one ready to use, works slick.

I would also like to say that in the city, some folks get a huge amount of leaves sometimes. Not always their own either, and have a hard time getting rid of them. Well for myself, I look at them leaves as gold.

What I like to do is wait till they are a bit wet. I then rake them into rows, not too high but just wide enough that I can run over them with my mower, as being wet they cut up twice as easy. Also doing this in the fall of the year my old mower blade is usually dull and a little duller isn't going to hurt anything.

Also if you have a great amount of leaves, too many to mulch and have a good size garden, just throw them right on top. Then just before you put that tiller away for it's winter nap, run it over your garden a few times, as that will chew up the leaves and come spring you will have a head start. I also do it again in the spring with my clean up, as I put in everything just before tilling. Once tilled up you won't even know you put anything in there, but your plants will sure thank you for it.

One thing I should mention here, some folks get their composting started by putting in a few handfuls of commercial fertilizer. Myself, I say that if you are going to do that, why even bother, as I figure the whole purpose of composting is to get the end results as organic as possible.

This is what you should remember. Leaves first, or wood sawdust, or shavings, then a wee bit of dirt sprinkled over the top, then a layer of grass cuttings and keep on repeating this all summer. The grass cuttings will take the place of the commercial fertilizer that some use.
That's it, that's all.

A Bit On
The Coming Of Spring

Well Christmas has long gone, the new year is on it's way and folks are busy paying off them credit cards. I sure am glad my wife and I got rid of ours years ago, I think we saved thousands of dollars by not having them. To our way of thinking, all they do is make others rich and our motto is, if we don't have the money we don't buy.

But that's not what this story is about. What it's about is that I have been giving some thought to my vegetable garden come spring. Too early you say, with Christmas just over, well not really, as one has to plan ahead. Old saying is, one can plan ahead just don't plan the results. I have two large gardens, one close to our house that has been well prepared since we moved here and another one aways from the house. The garden away from the house is OK for water early in the spring, but come summer when it gets hot, well, it's a challenge to get the water to it. One reason for it being so dry, is that the ground needs a lot more compost and things so that it will hold the moisture, and I am working on it.

So giving it some thought I came up with a plan. Until I get the one away from the house fixed up a bit more, I will plant my asparagus, strawberries and things that need water early in the season. That way the rains will look after things and when the hot weather arrives, I can then concentrate on the garden close to the house. Amazing what one can do with just a bit of thinking, and this is the time to do just that.

Last fall I picked up some good old cow manure and a few bails of straw. Some of the straw and manure I tilled in good before the ground froze. The rest of the manure I will spread around come spring, as soon as it thaws and then till it in good just before planting. I don't like to use chemical fertilizer if I can get away with it, as it don't give the fruit or vegetables the flavor that I am looking for. Even back on the farm we used manure, tons of it and when harvesting time came along, folks for miles around came to our place to buy, saying it was the best fruit they have ever tasted.

I would like to say one thing here though, on the subject of manure. Before you go and buy a load or two, kind of get to talking to the old farmer, or who ever and make sure of what he is feeding his cattle or other critters. Today they are feeding them tons of things that, you just don't need in your garden.

On another note I got out my stock of seeds that I put away last summer and lined them up on the table. Thing is one has to make plans of what they are going to plant and where, each year. I like to move things around, meaning not to plant the same thing in the same spot every year. I have found one can get away with it maybe two years in a row, but you will get nicer plants and more produce if you move them to different areas of your garden each year.

Usually I save my seeds from the past year but once in awhile I like to buy some new ones. There again, I have found that the seeds one gets from his or her plants each year looses a bit of their quality, so it's a good idea in picking up some new ones occasionally. One could just exchange the seeds though, if they had a neighbor that liked gardening, that would work too.

When it comes to buying my seeds, I like to buy from someone that has been around for a few years along with a good track record. Asking other gardeners or farmers is the best way to seek them out. It gives me a good feeling after I have figured what I am going to plant, not sure why, just been that way most of my life.

Well there you go, a bit on what's been on my mind and I hope it will help get you out and into the garden, as spring is just around the corner.

Farming
Yesterday And Today

Over the years working the land, one sometimes wonders how us old fellers managed to get things done. Especially if you compare the equipment we have in todays world with back when I was young. Today the idea is that farmers have to go big and rightly so I suppose, as the little guy has been pushed out, almost to extinction. I could go on here and stress what I think, should have been done back then and what should be done now, but what good would it do. But I do feel these three things are what caused the down fall of the farmers here in Canada and are worth mentioning.

One: Importing fruit and vegetables while ours is in season, should have never been allowed.

Two: The Fruit Marketing Board should have never been established.

And the big one number three: The Powers That Be should have stayed out of the the farming business, meaning, so many rules and regulations which put the little guy right out of business.

Now in saying this, remember, this is my opinion only and one would have had to have lived through the early years, to fully understand what I am saying.

But getting back to tools and equipment in the early days. On our farm we had two tractors, both Ford 8N's, along with numerous implements.

George Walters

Every day would start off just a bit before daylight and each day would end a bit after dark. Hot sun, dust, dirt, wind, rain, cold, snow, insects, you name it, never stopped the farmers of years past. If one looks back they were quite amazing people, never complaining about the hardships, as it was what we loved to do. Well, maybe some grumbled a bit, like myself.

Here where we live now, things have slowed down for my wife and I, but for the long and short of it, our hearts are still in farming. We still have our gardens and property to keep up, just now it's on a smaller scale, which is a good thing.

The tools one has now is a bit different, as the tractors are no longer needed, discs, plows and things are all gone. But there is a few things that will always be needed if one wants a good garden.

Awhile back I had a fellow drop by and asked, what he should buy so that he could get a vegetable garden to growing.

"Well," I said, "if you got a good size garden, a small good used or new tiller would be handy, but you can get by without it, you being a bit younger than me.

The next thing is go and buy yourself a good pointed mouth shovel, buy one with a good hickory or ash handle, not those plastic ones that are out there today, as they won't last you a week.

A couple stiff tooth rakes will be needed I suppose, to level off the ground before planting and I would also recommend a good stiff tooth, hand cultivator, they usually come with four teeth. What I did with mine, that I had for years, was take out two teeth which made it great for working up in between the rows and things.

Two more items would be, a good Axe, along with a pick, and again, all with good wooden handles.

The most important thing you are going to buy for gardening and I want to stress this, is a piece of equipment that goes back to the beginning of time. Without it your gardens will be over come with weeds. A piece that will toughen the young hands, will build muscles in your arms and shoulders and once you have used it for awhile, you will never go into the garden without it. That item is a hoe.

The best hoe that I have ever owned was my old Dad's. It has a hickory handle and is light as a feather. In the early days the blade was a bit longer than it was high but my Dad came up with the idea of rounding off the top edges. He also took it one step further and sharpened it up both sides, so now he could tip the hoe on edge and get into them hard to get spots, between the plants.

Yep I would feel lost with out mine and usually it goes where I go. It also comes in handy for when visitors drop by, as it gives one something to lean on while chatting.

So there you have it, a bit on how this old feller feels about farming, now and yesteryear, along with some gardening ideas thrown in for good measure.

Asparagus

Asparagus, now there is a plant that sure makes my mouth water. When cooked up with the right ingredients, it can be one of the tastiest treats to come out of ones garden each and every spring.

Harvest asparagus around 5 to 8 inches in length by cutting or snapping them off.

To cut a shoot, run a knife under the ground where the shoot emerges. Since the cut is below ground, it will still be necessary to snap the stem before cooking. Cutting may damage some shoot tips that have not emerged. That is why many horticulturists recommend snapping. To snap a shoot, bend it from the top toward the ground, doing that the shoot will then usually break off just a touch below the ground. Once it is cut and brought in the house, it is washed in cold fresh water and lightly boiled till tender, then drained. Then get to melting some real butter, add fresh crushed garlic and mix together. A touch of sea salt and ground pepper is then added and when done, put in a wrap of some kind with grated cheddar cheese, mm-mm good. Don't over cook it though as you will loose a lot of its goodness.

In growing asparagus it can't be easier. Thing one has to remember is making sure he or she gets a good amount of roots when buying. The lower the amount of roots, the longer it will take them to get established. Even with good roots it will take you around two years before you get to eating very much.

Asparagus is one of the first fresh vegetables to come into the house each spring. My wife sets out by the garden watching and waiting each year and when it shows itself for the first time you can see the smile come over her face. She sure loves the stuff I will say that, and me too for that matter. As I said try and buy the ones with the most roots you can find or if you know someone that grows their own, maybe ask for a few. Old saying is, you don't have nothing to loose and everything to gain.

The best time of year for planting these things are in the spring I have found. Some folks like the fall of the year, but being an old farmer I found spring plantings to be the best for everything other than garlic. Garlic likes the winter to get going and it also has a better taste than if it was planted in the spring.

Reason I like spring plantings is that they have all summer to get their roots established, simple as that.

Once you get your new asparagus plants, find a spot in full sun that won't be disturbed for years to come. Look ahead, as you don't want to have to dig them up if you don't have to. I shouldn't talk though, as that's just what I did. I had mine just coming up nicely and had to move them as I put in a row of raspberries and well, I think you know what happened, yep, the berries took over. So if you don't want your wife to be giving you the look all spring, make sure you plan ahead.

"Hmm, wonder what she is going to do, my wife that is, when I tell her I am moving my raspberries come next spring and that the asparagus could have been left alone?"

Asparagus grows pretty good in any type of well-drained soil but will not tolerate poorly drained soil. A deep loam or sandy loam is best, which we have a lot of here in the north.

Select a location on the edge of the garden or nearby that does not interfere with annual garden tillage and management.

The nice thing about asparagus is that it will keep on coming up each spring for around 10 to 15 years, can't beat that huh?

One other thing, try and keep your Ph in your vegetable gardens between 6.5 and 7.0, just a tip I have found that worked quite well for me over the years. Good idea to put one of them sensors on your Christmas shopping list, that way you can test your soil every spring and fall.

I would also like to say that Asparagus love to grow near, Basil, Carrots, Parsley and Tomatoes.

They get discouraged if you plant them beside, Chives, Garlic, Leeks and Onions.

So there you have it, a bit on Asparagus, one of the healthiest vegetables one can eat. Some say why grow my own, as it is so cheap each spring in the stores, well, my way of thinking is, I like to know what I am eating.

From Laura's recipe book. How to prepare asparagus, I love it.

Asparagus Recipes
One

Cut off the green ends and chop up the remainder of the stalks. Boil until tender and season with salt and pepper. Have ready some toasted bread, in a deep dish. Mix together equal parts of flour and butter to a cream and add to this slowly, enough of the asparagus water or clear water to make a sauce and boil this up. Put the asparagus on the toast and pour over the sauce. Just gotta try it!

Two
Cooked Asparagus

Ingredients:
2 pounds of asparagus
boiling water
1 tsp of salt

Wash the asparagus thoroughly and tie in a bundle, or into individual bundles. Place bundles upright with stems down in just enough boiling water to cover the thick part of the stalks, add salt and cook for 10 minutes or until stalks are tender. Once done arrange bundles in water so tips are covered and cook for 5 minutes longer. This way the tops don't over cook.

To serve, season with pepper and butter. Once on a plate, melt a wee bit of cheddar cheese, pour it over the top of the cooked asparagus. Yep, your in heaven. Enjoy!

Friends And Rheumatism

It had been a wet cold spring and being a nice day Reg and myself decided to visit an old feller that lived alone up the road aways. I didn't mind as I got to ride in the buggy, along with listening to some of the tales that these two told when they got to talking.

In about an hour we arrived and I spotted old Jim, that's the fellers name, out by the barn. By looking at him I could see he was moving a bit slow and limping a bit on one leg.

"What's the matter with your leg?" I hollered, as we got closer.

"Oh....... darn rheumatism is got to taking over my one leg these days, and sure is playing heck with me. I guess it's the wet, cold spring we've been having, sure be glad when that warm dry air starts to move into our area."

"Won't be long as I could feel it on my face riding over here," I said.

"Hope your right there young feller, hope your right. Pull that rig of yours up over by the house there and come on in and have a coffee. I think I can scrounge up a cup of hot chocolate too."

Well I listened to these old fellers talking for an hour or two enjoying every minute, but as the old saying goes, all good things come to an end sooner or later, and we were soon back on the road headin' home.

Later on the next day I decided to see my good friend Grey Wolf, who lived aways from our farm back in the bush by a creek. Nice fellow and a very wise old man. I had a notion that maybe he might be able to come up with one of his home made remedies for Jim's bad leg. Sure would be nice if he could get some relief from his pain.

As I arrived, I could see Grey Wolf sitting on his porch whittlin' away on a piece of wood. He enjoyed whittlin' as he said, it took his mind to unchartered places. Meaning, on to things and places that he hasn't seen before. I tried it a few times, whittlin' that is, but it didn't take me anywhere, or should say not till I got a bit older. At any rate I got to telling him about old Jim and he smiled and said.

"Yep them bones can sure play with a persons mind, when one gets a bit older. The cause is a lot of hard work over the years and old bones just get a bit weaker and can't take the cold, wetness and things. I do have an old remedy we have used for over a hundred years. Maybe we should make some now, that way you will know how to do it on your own, if you happen to need it some day."

"Sounds good to me," I said.

"First thing we have to find is a good size cedar tree. I say good size as the part we need is the leaves and once the leaves are picked they don't grow back. No problem, we have lots around the cottage."

We found a nice tall one and Grey Wolf walked over to it and reached up to one of the branches. Just before he took a few leaves he asked.

"Big cedar we have a fellow that needs your help and your healing leaves are needed. If you so choose to let me have a few I will reward you this fall with two fish to help you thrive through the winter months."

With that he was quiet for a moment, then continued on with picking the leaves.

"Always ask the tree before using any part of it young one, if you don't the medicine won't work."

Well we got busy and he showed me how to grind up the leaves in an old wooden bowl. Once done, he warmed up some hog fat or lard on his stove and mixed in the leaves that I crushed up. I would say there would be equal amounts of both, one hand full of each, to make things simple.

Once done, he strained the potion through a clean cloth and put it in a can he had saved from supper a few days before. He tied a piece of cloth around the top and said.

"Take this to your friend, and tell him to rub it on his leg for three days, twice a day. Once when he gets up in the morning and once before going to sleep and wrap it with a loose fitting cloth of some kind."

I did what Grey Wolf said and when we went to visit old Jim a few weeks later, we seen he was walking without the limp.

"Guess that salve old Grey Wolf fixed for ya worked huh?"

"Yep, sure did and if I wouldn't have tried it and seen the results myself I would have never believed it. You tell your friend his help is much appreciated and that if there is anything he needs that I can help him with, to just let me know."

"Will do," I said.

You know a lot of old time remedies were used back in the olden days. Not so much in todays world, reason being that humans have invented some medicine on their own. Some is good, some is not, but I will say this, I think there is a cure for any ailment we might get throughout life, right at our doorstep using Mother Nature. Problem is, we didn't listen to our Elders and we don't know where to look. Food for thought, one might say.

Since I had a bit of space left on this page, let me share with you Grey Wolf's words on how he washes his hair. Just one more piece of wisdom that might save you folks a dollar or two.

What You Need...

a.. Baking soda
b.. Water

What You Do...

1. Get your hair wet.
2. Then, take a handful of baking soda, and rub it into your hair and scalp.
3. Rinse your hair thoroughly.
4. Continue to use baking soda to wash your hair, avoiding regular shampoo all together.

Note: Initially, your hair will probably feel quite dry, but after a few weeks, your scalp will begin to produce more natural oils, and your hair's softness will return.

Why This Works ...

Baking soda's gritty texture grabs and removes the dirt and excess oil from your hair and the loose skin cells from your scalp, without stripping your scalp of its much-needed natural oils (like commercial shampoos do). Overtime, this leads to a healthier scalp and healthier hair.

Benefits of Using Baking Soda as a Dandruff or Regular Shampoo...

a.. inexpensive
b.. no harsh chemicals
c.. cleans without removing natural oils
d.. fragrance-free

Fruit Trees Of The Past

Well spring is in the air and I have been doing a bit of thinking on my garden for this year. One thing I enjoy doing is sitting on the front porch and jotting down different things that I might get to doing throughout the growing season. You noticed I said might, as, well, I for one change my mind every so often.

Here where we live, all along our fence lines, we have lots of choke cherries and for the past couple years my wife and I have made jam out of them. I have to say they make one of the nicest tasting jams going. The reason they are so good for jam making is the dry, tart taste they have. If you take one or two in your mouth, they for sure will pucker you up and that is what you want. I like to pick a few of them when they have just turned red. I then take them and put them into the freezer till a bit later on in the summer. Once the berries on the trees get to turning dark in color, almost black, I then pick the rest that I will need, which is usually around three or four quart baskets.

We then take the first ones we picked out of the freezer, let them thaw and mix them with the over ripe ones. Reason for doing this is that, the not so ripe ones give it that zip' that we all look for, along with having more acid in them, which extends the shelf life of the jam. Simple ways of doing things and everything is natural with no additives.

Another real nice fruit that makes good jam is Blue Damson Plums. They are real tangy and pucker up the old mouth too. On our farm we had around ten trees of them and as soon as they came into season we were sold out almost immediately. The older folks were the buyers, as they knew what they were and how good they were.

We also made a lot of jam out of Crab Apples, as they make good jam too. We had quite a few trees of them, lined one lane-way which was about an acre long. Most of these fruits are all gone today and for most parts folks don't or didn't even know they existed, too bad too.

I remember one fall we had a bumper crop of Kieffer Pears. Not too many folks would think of using them, but back in the old days they were the best pear you could get for preserving. Well, I hated to see them all go to waste so the wife and I got to picking them. I had in my mind the year before in pulling the trees out, but something told me not to.

After a week of picking, we ended up with around five hundred six quarts and they looked great, didn't have a mark on them. Well we loaded up the old truck and come Friday we headed north to where our market was located. I unloaded them and put them all out on racks piled high. I put a good price on them as I figured a little is better than nothing. By the end of the day we didn't have one basket left. Sold the whole load and folks ordered more for the following week. I was really surprised as I didn't think there was that many folks out there anymore, that knew what kind they were. Needless to say I didn't pull the trees out that fall and for years after that I had folks asking me when they were going to be in season.

Yep there was a lot of good old fruit trees back in my days of farming and it's too bad folks today won't have a chance to try them out. One reason being, most folks are just too busy trying to make a living than to be bothered with doing up preserves anymore. Most say they figure a trip to the super market is easier and cheaper.

Well, they are probably right to some extent, but I will tell you this. You will never find the taste of quality fruit, from a supermarket, as if you got it right from the farmer or grew your own.

There you go, a few words on some tender fruit that has left us and for those that might still happen to have a few trees, all I can say is, look after them.

Beans

One item that has been on my mind lately, relating to gardening and things, is that I sure hope that the folks in and around the cities here in the north don't become to commercialized. I have seen it happen, time and time again with the small time towns being swallowed up and lost forever. Thing is, us folks up here in the north have our own way of doing things and in my mind it would be a shame to loose that way of living, if not the greatest loss ever. Only reason I mention this, is because I can already see a change in the way things are going and I gotta' say this, all change is not always for the best.

On the topic of different things to plant now, beans comes to mind. They are a real nice treat for them meals throughout the summer months and also can be brought in for the cold winter months.

For a start, one should dig a trench about a foot deep and around ten inches across, something like potatoes, but in this instance once the trench has been dug out, I like to take all the old leaves I can find, rotten is best. I then lay them down in the bottom of the trench and spread a few handfuls of fresh grass cuttings over the top, the grass cuttings is the nitrogen and the leaves are the potash and other things that the beans will be needing.

I don't use any commercial fertilizer anymore these days, as I enjoy getting a garden growing just by using what comes naturally. If you do have to use a commercial fertilizer though, remember this, always buy fertilizer that has equal numbers, like 10-10-10. Some would disagree, but then they are allowed their point of view too.

Good old cow manurer is good too, so if you have some of that, use it instead, provided you know where it came from and what the critters were being fed.

For beans though, don't use chicken manurer at this time, it gets hot as it has a lot of ammonia in it and will burn the roots. Not saying it isn't a good manurer, just that it has it's place lets say.

Once you get that done cover the leaves and grass cuttings in the trench with some of that nice worked up earth, you just tilled, you are now ready for the beans. The thing one has to remember is that, preparation is as important, if not more, than the planting itself. Now, once you get that done you are all set, providing it's the right time of year, which would be around the 24th of May here where I live in the north. You should keep an eye on the weather though, as some years you can plant a touch early, some you can't, as the earth just isn't warm enough. If you get the seeds into the ground too soon, well they will either just sit there till things warm up, or they rot and you will have to replant.

I would also like to say here that a day before I get to planting, I take my beans wrapping them in a wet cloth and then put them somewhere in a dark spot overnight. Once this is done, I get my hoe out and make a slight dip on the ground above where I dug the trench earlier.

I then get to planting my beans, which is about six inches or so apart and about an inch or so deep. Now give them a wee bit of a drink but don't over water them, as too much is worse than not enough. Also remember that beans hate their roots being disturbed after planting, kind of like us older fellers and gals, the older we get the more we like to be left alone, well, at least for me.

Now all them leaves that we put in the bottom of the trench will come into play throughout the warm growing days of summer and you won't have to do anything but enjoy and watch them grow. They should be ready in about ten weeks or so, depending on what type you planted and if you played your cards right.

Nice thing about beans you can get three enjoyments out of them, one being, you can pick them just after they get to size and eat them raw with a salad or two you can boil them and cover them with a real nice cheese sauce, my favorite. The third one, just leave a few until they harden in their pods, you will then have a few for winters eating and next years planting. Not to mention that they last for years and you will always have a healthy meal ready for the making.

Pole Beans love to grow near; Carrots, Corn, Cucumbers, Eggplants, Lettuce, Peas and Radishes.

They don't like growing near; Basil, Beets, Cabbage, Onions or Sunflowers.

Bush Beans love to grow near; Beets, Cabbage, Carrots, Celery, Corn, Cucumbers, Eggplant, Lettuce, Marigolds, Peas, Potatoes, Radishes, Rosemary and Strawberries.

They don't like growing near; Basil or Onions.

So there you go a bit about the way I feel on a few things and another healthy meal that will get you into the right frame of mind throughout them lazy days of summer.

Now, back to my front porch sittin' with my lovely wife.

Recipe For Bean Soup

1 pound dried navy or pea beans
6 cups water
1/4 pound cooked salt pork
1 large onion -- chopped
1 large carrot -- peeled, chopped
4 cooked sausage links -- scored
1 bay leaf
1 1/2 teaspoons salt
1/2 teaspoon freshly-ground black pepper
1/4 teaspoon crumbled thyme

Let beans sit in a pot overnight in salted water. Then in the morning rinse thoroughly with fresh water, take all ingredients put in a crock pot and cook on High for 4 hours. Then stir beans; turn heat control to Low and cook until done.

Stir beans with a wooden spoon and mash some of them against the side of the cooker to thicken soup. Taste beans; season with additional salt and pepper, if needed. Now only thing left is for a slice of homemade bread and you have yourself a supper not to be forgotten. Enjoy!

P.S., Humming Birds love the flowers on beans and help with propagation.

Grapes

A few years ago when we were farming, our main crop was grapes. First to be grown here in this country were the Concord, Niagara, Fredonia, Catawba, Agawam and Delaware. All these grapes grew well in Southern Ontario and they also grow pretty well up here were we live, if some protection is given to them throughout the months of January and February.

The kind I chose to plant, was Concords and Niagara's. They are a good healthy vine, will tolerate the cold, birds, and most diseases. If you like grape jelly or jams, these are for you. I should also say they make good wine, but most folks today switched over to the hybrids as the sugar content in the new varieties are quite a bit higher. In saying that though, if one would leave, lets say, the concords on the vine till they are just a touch over ripe, you would find they would get the same sweetness as the newer varieties, but times change along with the way folks think.

The only problem with bringing hybrids over to this country, is they are susceptible to birds and lots of diseases. But if you got the money and time, you can make out with them, they won't grow well up here in the north though, too cold.

The main thing with grapes is trimming them the proper way. I like to put them in rows, with steel posts about ten or fifteen feet apart or so. Then run two wires from post to post, one up and one lower.

The grape vine when mature will look sort of like a tree, having the main stock with four arms, two coming out of each side, one above each other. The arms you need to keep when trimming, are the ones with the buds close together and they should be cut back throughout the winter months. Here in the north, I would recommend you trim them in the early spring just before the bud starts to open, reason being, you might loose them with freeze back if you trim them too early.

After you get them trimmed, it's time to tie them to the wires to keep them from falling on the ground. A trellis will work good too, if you only want a couple vines or so. Make sure you get them tied up before the buds come out, as the tender buds can be broke off quite easily.

Once that is done, work up around the base of the vine a bit and give them some good old cow manure, or what ever you have available. About a quarter bushel per vine would be great. I don't like chemical fertilizer as I keep telling ya, but to each their own.

Here is a chart on what types of manure I like to use with certain crops.

Garden Type	Best Manure	When
Flowers	Cow, Horse	Early Spring
Vegetables	Chicken, Cow, Horse	Fall, Spring
Potato or Root Crop	Chicken, Cow, Horse	Fall, Spring
Blueberries	Cow, Horse	Early Fall Only
Grapes	Cow, Horse, Chicken	Fall, Spring
Fruit Trees	Cow, Horse, Chicken	Fall, Spring

The only other thing you will have to do, is sucker them, which means take off the growth that comes up from the bottom of the vine through spring. Once they start growing, just break them off by pushing them in a down ward motion, they will come off real easy.

Next thing is, just sit back and wait. If you planted Concords you should have a crop, late September. If you planted Niagara's you will have a crop around mid September. Might be a week later up here in the north depending on the year.

I should mention the Concords are blue grapes and the Niagara's are white, or some call them green grapes.

The Fredonia are also blue and a good eating grape, they also make excellent juice or jelly.

Agawam are red and good for wine along with the Catawba.

The Delaware are also red and prime grapes for wine, smaller berry and real sweet.

Points Of Interest

Plants that are beneficial to grapes are; basil, beans, peas, or blackberries. Keep radishes and cabbage away from grapes. Planting clover increases the soil fertility for grapes and chives with grapes help repel aphids.

So, that's all there is to having your own grapes, no excuse now for not having fresh grape jelly in the cupboard, for the cold winters days. Makes me hungry just thinking about it.

Concord Jelly Recipe

4 c. fresh grape juice
7 c. sugar
1/2 bottle liquid pectin

Sort, wash and remove stems from grapes. Place in a saucepan and add water. Cover and bring to a boil on high heat. Reduce heat to simmer for 10 minutes. Strain juice through cheesecloth. Measure juice in kettle and stir in sugar. Place on high heat, stirring constantly. Bring to a full rolling boil that can't be stirred down. Add pectin and return to full rolling boil. Boil jelly mixture for 1 minute. Remove from heat and quickly skim off foam. Pour jelly into hot jelly jars and seal. Should make around 10, eight ounce jars. Enjoy!

Not Just Any Bug

Y ears ago back on our old farm, we rented fifty acres of mixed fruit as
an extra. Between the rental and our own farm, I had in the back of my mind
we would have some extra fruit for market throughout the coming season.

Down at the rental property one day, I had just put in a good mornings
work and decided to go and sit under a big old maple tree to eat my lunch.
As I sat there I spotted this log which time had started to decay and I noticed
some bugs crawling over it. I got up and walked over to have a closer look.
I moved the log a bit and to my surprise it was hollow and there was
thousands of lady bugs inside it. After sitting there watching them for
awhile, eating my lunch, I rolled it back over and went about my work.

Later on in the season back on our farm, I got to noticing that we had a
real problem with Aphids. For the past few years I was trying to stay away
from pesticides to fight the insects, and the Aphids, well, I knew it was going
to be a problem.

I got to talking to my old Dad that night about what to do, and he said.
"You know that log you found with all the lady bugs?"
"Yep I remember."
"Well tomorrow, take a pail with a lid and bring back all you can."
"Why would I want to do that?" I asked.

37

"Well, lady bugs eat Aphids, they are their main source of food. We use to have lots of them here on the farms, but everyone around us has been spraying pesticides for so long, it has killed them all off. If your lucky, they might just fix your problem and some of mine too."

The next morning I dug up two pails and headed on down to the rental property. I rolled over the log and sure enough they were still there, by the thousands. Well I laid the pail down on its side and with my hand I pushed in all I could and filled the second one too. I put them in the cab of the truck with me and headed on back home.

Driving past Dads house I spotted him out under the tree reading a book, so I stopped and showed him.

"Well lets go and see what we can do," he said. "Maybe we can give Mother Nature a bit of hand." We jumped in the truck and while I was driving over to my farm, he had a look.

"Boy that is sure one mess of lady bugs.....can't rightly say, I ever seen that many all in one spot. That should get the job done just fine."

We pulled up in front of the old barn and walked out to the field. Dad took one pail and I took the other.

"Alright, about every fifty feet or so take out a handful and lay them up on a branch in the tree, and be a bit careful not to hurt them."

It took the better part of the afternoon to get them spread out in the orchard, but if it worked, it would be well worth the time.

"Now all we have to do is sit back and see what happens," said Dad.

"Do you really think it will work, as there is millions of them Aphids?"

"You just watch," Dad said.

Well in two weeks there wasn't an Aphid to be found and in a few weeks more, the trees that had lost some of their leaves due to the Aphids eating them, grew all new ones. That year we had the best crop of fruit you could ever ask for. Nice thing about it was, we never had to put a drop of pesticides on the trees that year, or for the next three years after that.

So, goes to show ya, with a bit of thinking and the help of nature, a major problem was fixed up. In my opinion, if I were asked, I would have to say that we would be a lot better off with out all the pesticides of today and years past. We might loose a bit of our crops, I realize this, but the rewards in the end would out number the loss I am sure.

What happens is, this old world produces some insects and things, that, can cause a farmer problems, but not too far behind them is another insect that preys on them. If left alone, for most parts a fellows problem looks after itself and the best part about letting it happen on its own, is we all eat a lot healthier and isn't that what should be happening.

Pretty hard to do in todays world though, as things have gotten messed up, but there is still some hope, we just need to bring back some common sense into our every day life.

Lawns And Other Things

I usually put my vegetable gardens in, around May 24th. Takes me two or three days to get it planted but if one thinks about it, that's not too much time to take out of a fellers life for what one gets out of it.

Some years has been pretty dry and with that happening one sure has to be on top of things with the watering. As soon as the seeds break ground and the plant starts to grow, one then can ease off the watering a bit, as once that happens the ground is shaded and the plants don't need as much.

Tomatoes through the dry season should be watered every third day if at all possible, as tomatoes love it hot and sunny, but they require lots of water.

Now for a bit on lawns. Over the years I have helped hundreds of folks grow nice lawns. One should remember that you don't have to go to extremes to have a nice lawn, I like to keep things simple.

After years of planting different lawns I would have to recommend Perennial Ryegrass mixed with a bit of clover. Being an old farmer we used to seed in between the grape rows and the fruit trees every year, as it would grow up full and rich with nitrogen. Then once up about halfway we would disc it under for a fertilizer, all organic and can't be beat. Of course we only used annual Ryegrass for that as it was a lot cheaper.

George Walters

Now though they have perennial Ryegrass, which is my first choice for a nice lawn. Grows well in the shade, in the sun and also under trees, it also resists many insects and diseases.

Just before planting the seed though, a few things have to be done. First I recommend that you put down a good 10-10-10 fertilizer, unless you have a good source of fresh cut grass clippings. If you have an abundance of clippings handy, sprinkle them all over the area you are working with, as it will do the same job as the chemical fertilizer, if not better. If you do use chemical fertilizers remember to keep them three numbers on the bag all the same, reason being, all the ingredients in the bag will then be equal and that is what you are lookin' for in a good lawn. Don't need one number fighting against another.

Now work your lawn up good with a tiller and level it as smooth as you can with a good stiff tooth rake, don't till it too deep, not necessary and just makes for a whole lot of extra work.

Once done, you can hook a long hardwood board to a couple ropes if you like and just drag it across where you raked, that will flatten it nicely for your seeding. After that it's time to do some seeding.

I think every one should have one of those hand spreaders with a crank on the side, they are relatively not too expensive these days and easy to use, also it broadcasts the seeds down more evenly and one doesn't get to over doing it, as good seed is expensive.

Get yourself in a walking mode and get to it. An easy way to figure on how much seed to put down is simple actually and it goes like this.

If you can see it from a standing position, you have the right amount put down.

"Simple huh?"

Now once that is down it is a good idea to go over it with a light roller. Worth saying twice, a light roller. I am kind of partial to one of those that you fill with water as you can fill it with whatever amount you want, which for this job would be about half-full. You want to push the seeds down into the new tilled soil, but not too far, quarter inch is sufficient.

For years I had a small cement one and it worked great till it eventually just fell apart, caused from me dropping it off my old truck one too many times while loading it. Tried fixing it, but it just never was the same, guess it was mad at me or something.

Anyways, after the seed is spread and you go over it once with the roller, I then recommend covering it with either a peat moss, or again grass cuttings. It not only holds the moisture for the seeds to germinate, but also gives them much needed nitrogen in the beginning. It also hides the seeds a bit from them pesky birds.

Once you get that all done, I recommend you get yourself a glass of home made lemonade, get out your most favorite chair and do some front porch sittin' and watch it grow.

40

But maybe I am jumping ahead here a wee bit too fast. As soon as you get it covered, the seed that is, give it a good watering. This is very important and water it faithfully every other day until it starts to grow, it won't take long.

Spring is the best time of the year to get grass growing, but summer is OK too, you just have to water more till it gets established.

As I said before, my most favorite lawn seed is Perennial Ryegrass mixed with a bit of clover and with that I would like to say a bit about clover.

Years ago there were lots of clover lawns but they got phased out as some folks didn't like the bees bothering them when the clover came into flower. Myself I think it is a plus, the more bees the better as long as they are Honey or Bumble Bees, not a great lover of them Wasps, Yellow Jackets or Hornets, although they do have a right on this old earth, just as we do and they have a job to do like gathering various insects, many of which are plant parasites.

But if they take up homesteading in my garden which they do occasionally, well, lets say I do all I can in helping them move.

There is other ways to get a new lawn and that is using sod, which I will discuss in another story. One last thing, now that I showed you how to plant a nice lawn, do me one favor, let it grow naturally without all the pesticides.

Now...... go and get that cool glass of lemonade, sit back and enjoy!

Summary For Perennial Ryegrass.

   * Commonly mixed with Kentucky Bluegrass or White Clover to improve wear and tear, allowing growing in shade, and speed up establishment.
   * Requires about 10 days to germinate.
   * Shiny, medium to dark green.
   * Fine to medium in texture.
   * Does not spread laterally.
   * Tolerant of cold and warm temperatures.
   * Germinates rapidly, making it useful if you need to get a lawn off to a fast start.

Good Food

Seems when spring arrives each year I am ready for it. I suppose the cold is what gets to me the most as every once in awhile a winter comes by that is long, wet, and cold with hardly no sunshine. Although it doesn't bother me and I enjoy being outside in the fresh air, one has to learn to dress for it.

At any rate one plant that gets to growing in the early spring, which is great for salads and things, is the dandelion. I know some folks figure they are just a weed and a nuisance. Not to mention how some folks spend hundreds of dollars a year just to get rid of them in their lawns. Myself I would have to say they have been highly underrated and a lot of folks have had their minds swayed into thinking they are a bad thing, which in my eyes isn't true.

For my wife and I, we can't wait till they start coming up, as we use pretty well every part of them. In the early spring we like to get the flowers just when they start to open, when you can see just a wee bit of the yellow. We pick them and on a Saturday which is our home made pizza day my wife puts them all over the top of our pizza, just before it goes into the oven. I got to tell you it is mouth watering good.

Another part is the leaves and one should pick them when they are young, at least that is the time we like them the best. The older they get the more bitter they get. I pick a few hat fulls and the wife puts them in salads, on sandwiches or along with just about anything else we eat. Can't be beat in my books, an so.... healthy for ya.

Now here is where most folks stop, but not us, as the best part is yet to come, the roots. Yep the roots. I like to dig them in the fall of the year if possible but the spring is good too. I dig them up and bring them into the house for the wife, where she washes them and spreads them out on a drying rack. Ours is the oven, as it is heated with propane and with the pilot light going all the time it is a perfect spot to dry things like that.

Usually once a week she makes bread, so while the oven is on she bakes the roots along with the bread as not to waste propane. You can tell when they are cooked to perfection as your house will start to smell like chocolate.

Once that is done she then lets them cool a bit and when she has a free moment she puts them into a coffee grinder and grinds them all up. She then puts them into an old coffee can with a good lid and stores them away.

Now when coffee time comes around, which is about 2:00 PM each afternoon, out they come. The wife then takes half ground coffee and half ground dandelion roots and mixes them together. I have to say it's my most favorite time of the day.

I like to dig my roots right on the edge of a bush we have on our property, as the mulch from the trees over the years is just right for what they need to grow and grow they do. Just another reason not to cut down all the trees around ones home.

The nice thing about the dandelions here in the north, is that they still have all the vitamins and minerals in them. One thing you have to remember though, make sure where you pick them that they haven't sprayed them with pesticides and things, as sure wouldn't want anyone to get sick. Here where we live now, we don't use any pesticides at all, so whatever is growing on our property we know is safe to eat, meaning dandelions and veggies from our gardens.

A few things that the dandelions are good for health wise are; ones liver, balances the blood sugar in your body, helps with digestion, lowers cholesterol, lowers blood pressure, cleanses the skin and even helps in weight reduction.

Another good thing to do is dig up a few dandelions and plant them around your gardens as they produce pollen for lady bugs, lacewings, and other predators and parasites which is necessary for a good garden. They also will discourage potato bugs from coming into your garden. I am sure there is more but that's a few that I know of.

Well, there is a bit about the yellow flower of spring. I hope every one will at the very least try it on a pizza once throughout the growing season as I am sure, you will be pleasantly surprised.

I also hope it gets folks minds to realizing that they are a good plant, not a bad plant, and that Mother Nature has a lot to offer, if we just stop and take a minute to do some research.

Enjoying Winter

Well when winter strikes I suppose gardening is probably the furthest thing from folks minds. While writing this story with outside temperatures of around 17 degrees old scale, one would sure think nothing would be growing in the garden that's for sure. But sitting at my desk looking out I got to noticing a few green shoots coming up from some old potatoes and my garlic I planted last fall. I bet they got a shock with todays weather, being so cold. But not to worry, they will be back once the old sun gets around to warming things up a wee bit.

If I was back on the fruit farm now at this time of year, I would be out there trimming grapes. I usually start a few weeks before Christmas and work steadily at it till spring, as it takes a couple of fellers a bit of time to get through a hundred acres. Thinking back, for most folks it would be quite a job out there in the cold, but for me I actually enjoyed it.

For amusement while working out there by myself, I got to watching different critters running around and my old dog Trixy, well she was the most entertaining of them all, as she loved to catch mice. She would dig them up with her nose, throw them in the air and then if it was around dinner time, well, you know the rest. I got to say she was a good old dog and I sure miss her, even after all these years, amazing how a feller can get attached to things like that.

Up here around our home though I wouldn't recommend any trimming on the grapes till March, as we get some real cold weather and if trimmed too early the vines freeze back which could cause you to loose a few.

Even though we don't have the farms anymore I have to admit I still get the urge to get out there once in awhile, but downsizing from a hundred acres to five or six vines, well, lets just say the urge passes pretty quick these days.

Through the winter months I kind of stay close to home and work out in my shop or here at my desk. The thing that keeps me most fit is carrying firewood for the old shop stove and keeping the wood furnace stoked up in the house. I enjoy it though and nothing is nicer than working away in the shop on a cold day or sitting in a nice warm house heated by wood, typing up a story or two. Old friend of mine always says.

"Just because I can."

There is lots of different things though that can keep a person busy, like sending away for different seed catalogs and browsing through them. Kind of gets the old mind out of the gray days and back into the warm sunny days. I got to say though I don't usually buy too much from them catalogs, as over the years I have saved my seeds from different plants that I have grown from years past. Saves a few dollars doing it that way and also I know what I am getting.

What I usually do is buy a couple different kinds each year and if one happens along that is exceptionally good, well I either keep a few seeds, or a shoot and bring them inside come fall. Then come spring around the middle of March, I get them started in some potting soil and after the 24th of May outside they go.

Another thing folks can do to pass the time, is to take some of your Florida Grapefruit seeds and put them in the fridge for a few days. That is if you haven't had them keeping in the fridge already. Then put them into some potting soil and come spring you will have a nice size plant and if your real lucky, in a few years you will have a grapefruit or two of your own. Use only Florida ones though as the others seem to be harder to get growing, but your choice. I have also found you can't beat the taste of Florida Grapefruit in season, just something about them that gets my mouth to watering.

Another nice thing about winter is the wife and I get into all the preserves we did up out of our garden throughout the growing season. Just a bit of work through the nice weather and one has some pretty tasty things to chew on through them cold days, also real healthy for you too.

So guess that's it, hope you all survive the winters from here on in and don't let them dreary days get you down, as there is always something one can do, just have to use ones imagination. Least that is what my lovely wife keeps telling me.

Ashes To Ashes

Ashes to ashes, no I am not done for yet, but did one ever take a close look at, wood ashes. You know for years folks have used ashes for all kinds of different things. For me and my family on the farm they were an all purpose item and in saying that I figured maybe I would share a few of them with ya.

The first is, that years ago when working on equipment us old farmers had a tendency of getting ones hands in a bit of grease, oil and gas now and then, or at least that's what my lovely wife tells me. She hates the smell of gas but for me now, I love the smell of it, or for that matter even oil and grease, just something about them that makes me feel good.

"Must be a man thing, the wife says, but keep it out of the house."

Anyways, for the grease on our hands and things there is nothing better than a bit of soft ashes. Just a handful or so will take the smell and things right off in no time flat.

Another use is for grubs in your front lawn and things. Amazing huh? Well all you do is just take the ashes out of your stove and sprinkle them over the infected area. Once done if you sprinkle a wee bit of water over it, not much, just enough to wet it lightly, it will get to working a lot faster, no pesticides needed.

Treading along here, another good use for the ashes is putting them around your fruit trees to keep the mice from chewing on the bottoms, or any tree for that matter that them pesky critters take a notion on eating.

One can also mix up some ashes with a bit of water and spray your vegetables and things with it. What I usually do to make things simple, is I just take about four handfuls of the ashes and a half a pail of water, mix it with a stick or something and just sprinkle it over the vegetables or what ever I am having a problem with at the time. Works great, as the ashes have a cutting affect to the smaller insects and, well, they just don't bother with the plants. Oh and I should mention here that it doesn't hurt them good old earth worms, as I had a worm tell me that one day, while I was down on my hands an knees planting seeds.

Wood ashes can also be used to raise the pH in the soil and over a few years I have found it works excellent. Only thing is, if you do use wood ashes on your garden, use them throughout the winter months so they work their way down into the soil and come planting season they won't cause you any problems. Problem being, that fresh ashes can slow down your seeds a bit while breaking ground, just something to keep in mind.

Years ago Laura the lady of the house used to use the ashes in the making of Lye soap, and I would think it would be probably better for folks than all the stuff we are using now in todays world. Going to have to dig around and see if I can find that recipe for you, that she left behind, as I got her real old cook book and it has tons of different things in it.

Another good use for ashes is to cover the leaves on your raspberries in the fall of the year, as it sure keeps the deer and rabbits from eating them. They sure put up their nose when they come to feed.

When it comes to ice storms, there is nothing better than to take a bucket of ashes and sprinkle them on top of the ice in the driveway, sidewalk or where ever you don't want to slip. It also is good to carry a bag in the trunk of the car in case you get into a slippery situation, just make sure they are not hot coals when you put them in there. I know you all knew that.

We also used to put ashes in a barrel which was filled with water, we would stir it up a little and let it settle. Once settled we would then use the clear water, about a cupful to the clothes wash water, it worked great.

Last but not least there isn't anything better than lye soap made with ashes, if one happens onto a patch of poison ivy.

Well there you go, a few uses for good old wood ashes, and to think some folks thought they were no good for anything.

Strawberries

You know, I was taught years ago that self respect was described as liking yourself the way you are, it does not require that we compare ourselves to others I was told, and over the years I have always remembered that. Only reason I mention it is that I have woven my life around what I was taught and it has sure helped me throughout my life. Especially when it came to farming, as we did things a bit different and if one had self respect down solid, it meant they could go about their work without worrying or thinking what other folks thought. As I got older I took what I was taught in my younger years, along with a bit of my own ideas and put them together. I have to say I was never afraid to try something new or experiment with things.

I for one, after selling the farms and moving here to the north, have actually found a lot of folks thinking the way I do. I have to say it gives me a good feeling seeing that, as I had it figured a lot of it was forgotten in todays world. Not sure why I got to talking about them things, but like a lot of things I write, they just come to me and I don't question them very often. Just needed saying I suppose. OK, now that's out of the way I will get on to the strawberries.

One year I ordered some new strawberry plants and had them shipped to me by mail, from an old friend of mine. He grows them by the thousands so figured if anyone would know a good kind to plant up here in the north, he would. One has to just bite the bullet once in awhile and do these things if they want a few of the good things in life. Thing is, to get a crop producing, one has to get them in the ground, thinking about it in ones mind doesn't get the job done. It takes two years to get a good taste.

The strawberries I ordered were called Cavendish, a real nice berry that comes on mid to early summer, depending on how the season goes. When one buys plants they should take in what kind of weather they have in your area, as it will greatly affect your crops.

The first thing in getting ready for the new plants is to get the ground worked up well. Once that is done I like to dig a trench about a foot deep and throughout the bottom, place in some old compost, or you could use a bit of cow manure if it is handy, a little goes a long way. Just skim the bottom and then put around a two inch layer of dirt on top, once that is done you can get to planting, this will promote root growth which is what you want at this point.

Once that is done you need to put down some nice straw, which goes around the plants. This will hold the moisture and also keep the berries from rotting, which would happen, if left on the ground. About a week before my berry planting I had a couple projects on the go here in my woodworking shop, so I kept the pine shavings and put them around the strawberries instead of straw. If you happen on some shavings, just make sure its pine and not oak or walnut shavings, as they might end up killing your new plants.

Some say in the first year you should take off the flowers as it promotes growth for the new plants and rightly so, but I left a few on, as my yearnin' for a taste clouded my better judgment a bit.

Once the berries are growing and some runners start to strike out from the mother plant, one should take these and cover a portion of them with some dirt. Doing this will start new plants and that is what you want to happen throughout the growing season. In a year you should have a row about two feet wide or better.

How many plants a person buys, depends on if one wants them for their own use or to sell. Say for a family of four, I would recommend about twenty five plants. That should satisfy your cravings for one winter after all done up and put in the freezer. That's the way we like them.

Nothing seems to bring in friends more than fresh raspberries or strawberries throughout the lazy days of summer. Myself, I love to put them right in a bowl after picking and lightly cover them with fresh cream and just a touch of sugar. Hard to get fresh raw cream now a days though as farmers aren't allowed to sell it anymore. Too bad too as my mouth gets to watering just thinking about that fresh raw cream. Got to say here one thing on the subject of raw milk, cream and butter. I was raised on it for most my life and it never ever caused me any trouble health wise. The whole secret to good raw milk can all be said in one word, cleanliness.

How deep to plant your new berry plants?

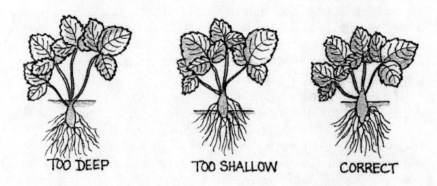

TOO DEEP   TOO SHALLOW   CORRECT

Strawberries love to grow beside; Bush Beans, Lettuce, Onions, Radishes and Spinach. They get upset when they are planted beside, Cabbage or Potatoes.

Final note, nothing is more healthier for you than to grow your own vegetables and fruits, so why not give your body the respect it deserves.

How We Freeze Strawberries? Here You Go...

Halve or slice strawberries into a bowl. Sprinkle 1/2 cup sugar over each quart of strawberries. Stir gently until the sugar is dissolved. Be careful not to damage the strawberries. Pack into freezer container, seal tightly and freeze. It's that simple, and come winter, you are in for a treat. Enjoy!

Horseradish Roots

Y ou know, another vegetable I love to grow is Horseradish Roots. If you never tasted home made horseradish you are missing out on something special.

One though has to remember in getting ready to plant horseradish, that it is a perennial, meaning, it will keep on coming back every year. Kind of like getting a bonus in with your pay check every week, my way of looking at it. For myself I don't buy anything other than perennials anymore when it comes to flowers and certain kinds of veggies, just for that reason.

In getting ready to plant horseradish one should also keep this in mind, you want to make sure you plant them in a spot where they won't be disturbed. The nice thing about horseradish root is that, the pH in your soil can be anywhere from around 5 to 7, which gives plenty of lea-way. A quick way to find out the pH of an area is to look to see if there are any house hydrangeas already growing in the area. If so observe the color of its flowers. A soil pH of 6 or below will produce blue flowers, while a soil pH of 6.8 or higher will produce pink flowers. If you don't have a hydrangea, might be a good idea picking one up and planting it near your veggie garden.

Back on the farm I had a row of horseradish around twenty feet long and after a period of two years we had more than we could use and eventually we were digging it and selling it on the farmers market. I did bring some with me when we moved here to the north, but somehow it got misplaced I guess and never did find it. A year later though I was down at Louie's place a real good friend of mine and he dug me up some plants from his garden, got more than I need now. Old Louie has passed on but as long as I am walking around, he will never be forgotten, great fellow.

You can plant horseradish either in the fall of the year, or in the spring, don't really matter, but what does matter, is that it has had a taste of cold weather before planting. If you plant in the spring make sure it has felt cold or if your not sure, wrap the root in a paper bag, like the old lunch bags and put them in the fridge over night.

Then, when you do get ready for planting make sure you dig a good size hole for each root, reason being is that with any root crop it is essential that it has room to move freely.

Here again I can't stress enough, just before putting the roots into the ground, put a hand full of good compost or manure to each hole, cover lightly with more soil and then plant. Taking the time to do this each and every time you are planting, will give the plants the edge they need in getting started. Got to kind of think of them as being your young ones, you wouldn't just send them out into the world without a bit of help.

Once planted it won't be long before you see them sprouting up above the ground seeking out the old sunshine. Don't worry too much if they wilt a bit, as being so young and tender they seem to do this and in no time they will straighten out all on their own.

The first year crop is the tastiest I have found, but just remember it's best not to dig them till after the first frost, some folks do, but I like the taste better later on, to each their own though.

When you get to digging your first years crop, that's the time to split the roots a bit and replant for next year. This way you won't have to keep on buying new plants every year. Thinking back there wasn't too many plants that I ever had to buy more than once, as if there was any possible way of saving seeds, grafting, or you name it, I did it. Why not make use of what you have, also it gives me great pleasure to be able to do it.
One might say, "Just because I can." A good friend of mine came up with that saying.

I should say if you happen to see your horseradish the first year not doing so well, which shouldn't be the case if you did what I recommended in the beginning, you can add a bit of low nitrogen fertilizer around each plant, lets say a spoonful, no more. Myself, and again I keep on saying this, when buying fertilizer, always keep them three numbers on the bag the same. My favorite is 10-10-10 if I don't have any grass cuttings, as it can be used for everything, vegetable gardens, flower gardens, fruit trees and even the lawn.

Horseradish also likes to grow near potatoes and fruit trees. There is a spray one can make from the roots of horseradish which helps with the prevention of fungal diseases and potato bugs. It is especially useful against brown rot in apple trees along with numerous other problems that might arise in ones gardens.

Take one cup of roots and put in a food processor till finely chopped. Combine this with 16 ounces of water in a glass container and let soak for 24 hours. Strain liquid, discard the solids. Now mix the liquid with 2 quarts of water and spray, that's all there is to it and no dangerous pesticides needed.

Well you should be all set now as nothing is more tastier than a home-made batch of creamy horseradish on top of a good hot dog.

One last note, don't forget to take a bit of time, put out a chair near your garden and just let the smells and good feelings come over you, that's what it's all about.

Good old time Horseradish Recipe;

Grate very fine a couple small horseradish roots. Taking two tablespoons, mix a teaspoon of salt, and four tablespoons of cream. Stir briskly and add slowly a wine glass of vinegar.

"One More? Oh...OK."
Horseradish Sauce;

Two teaspoons of preferably home made mustard, but a good store boughten one will do. Two teaspoons of white sugar. Half a teaspoon of salt and a gill of vinegar, (Oh forgot, old way of saying things,) half a cup of vinegar. Mix together and pour it over your horse-radish. Great with roast beef.

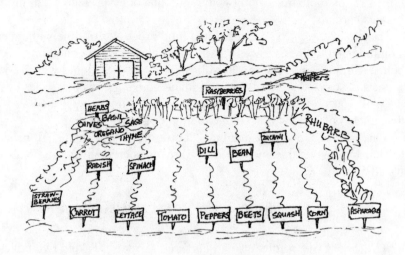

Summer Happenings

Summer is usually a very exciting time for my wife and I as we love to be outside chatting to folks, and, well just doing what we enjoy.

Usually my tomatoes around mid summer needs some attention especially if it has been a slow year in starting. Seems when that happens they grow more foliage than they do tomatoes, which in turn slows down the tomatoes from ripening. So when that happens they need a bit of trimming so the sun can get at them, an old trick my Dad taught me years ago.

Also every once in awhile the tomatoes get to rotting a wee bit on the bottoms and turning black, caused by a wet season and, a heavy amount of leaves. To help this problem, trimming is about the only remedy other than spraying with a fungicide. If I have to spray though I don't turn to the man made fungicides of today, I use the mixture I make out of horseradish roots which I told you about in the story before this one.

But for most parts if a problem arises we usually still make out pretty good, as I haven't seen a year yet that my lovely wife hasn't been busy putting things into jars.

She just doesn't do up tomatoes though, jams and jellies are pretty high up there on the list of things too. Usually some friends drop by from Niagara and bring us some grapes, peaches and plums, which are then either put in jars or the freezer. I always feel better knowing the cupboards are full and fresh fruit and veggies are in the jars when old man winter hits. Not sure why folks don't do more of that, but then again I suppose it's because they are too busy working at their jobs, especially in todays world. Too bad too.

My wife and I enjoy the produce we grow, main reason is, we know what is in them. Don't know if you knew it or not, but one tomato should have around 57 vitamins and minerals in each one. Thing is, today most of them only have around five or six. Problem is most are grown now in greenhouses or in soil that just don't have the minerals in it anymore. Folks have been putting so many chemicals on the ground, that any benefits from the fruit are gone pretty well.

The big thing though, is the pesticides. The soil of today has so much of it in it, that one has a hard time finding any vegetables or fruit pesticide free. That's the nice thing of growing your own, or knowing some one that does.

Nothing better than having a nice thick, flavorful slice of a tomato, right from your own garden, that when bitten into just brings the old taste buds alive, that's the way it should be.

On another note, I love peppers and over the years each fall I love to take the seeds after my wife cuts them open and dry them for the following year. Simple thing to do and also saves one a bit of money. I dry my seeds on some paper and then put them in a small jar with a teaspoon of sugar or rice, which keeps the moisture from getting into the seeds. I then like to keep my seeds in the dark, very dry, at a low, even temperature.

Also if you have a few plum, or peach pits, dry them and then just before the frost hits, bury them about three or four inches in the ground and leave them there till spring. The cold up here in the north will crack the pits and you should have some new seedling trees come spring. I put them in one spot so I don't forget where, around ten or so, that way I am sure of getting at least one or two trees. Once they start in the spring dig them up and move them to wherever you want. Simple and easy on the pocket book. Don't forget though, more than one fruit tree is needed to produce fruit, they love company.

Well couldn't just finish this story without one last bit on seeds. Here is a list for you just in case you want to store your seeds. It will let you know how long you can keep them, providing you store them correctly. They are all numbered in years.

So in saying that it would be a good idea to mark the year on each package of seeds, at least that's the way I do it, as I have a hard enough time remembering what mischief I got into throughout one day.

Seed Storage In Years

Asparagus 3 , Beans 3, Beets 4, Broccoli 3, Brussels sprouts 4, Cabbage 4, Carrot 3, Cauliflower 4, Celery 3, Swiss Chard 4, Chicory 4, Sweet Corn 1, Cucumber 5, Lettuce 5, Parsley 1, Pea 3, Pepper 2, Pumpkin 4, Radish 4, Rutabaga 4, Spinach 1, Squash 4, Tomato 4, Turnip 4, Watermelon 4. Enjoy!

Spring And Gardening

Well I got to tell you folks, when spring arrives each year I am sure ready for it. Moving to the north is sure something to behold, I will say that. I have been to a lot of different countries throughout my life but haven't really seen one that has been better than my own back yard. Just something about it up here that gets a fellows blood just a flowing, makes you wanna get out of bed every morning.

I enjoy all the seasons though, not just spring. Summer and fall are just as nice, but when winter hits I got to say, that I am sure glad I am heating with wood. Through my eyes one couldn't ask for a better heat for aches and pains of a body that might be getting a touch older. Now I am saying a touch older now, don't want you folks to get to thinking I am over the hill or something like that.

But getting back to spring, each year I get to talking to one of my buddies in Michigan and he usually has a sure fire method of tellin' when spring is arriving. Here is how that phone call would go.

"Well George, seen some turkeys that were fanning out in the field by the house this morning, along with some woodchucks, starlings and robins. Seems to me that they all drop by for a visit around the eighth of March. Temperature don't seem to bother them though, as it is 24 degrees here this morning, so I would have to say they know something more than I do."

Of course the conversation wouldn't stop there, but that gives you a drift of how different folks think about things. Now in the temperature department you have to remember he is talking Fahrenheit, not Celsius when he says 24 degrees. You know I never switched to metric when it came to Canada, reason being was simple. I just liked it the way it was and figured there was no good reason to change. Now remember that's just me.

One of the first things I get to doing come spring, as soon as the snow has melted, is pick up all the branches that has gotten broke off throughout the winter. Things like that bother me for some reason, as I can't just let something lay around if it needs picking up. I always remember my old Dad saying while out for a walk.

"If you come along something that needs doing in your travels, do it George, as it will save you steps in the coming days and every extra step we take uses up energy and wastes time."

For example, I could be heading to the garden out back and might happen on something laying around that shouldn't be there. Well instead of just passing it by leaving it for later, I pick it up, and well got two jobs done for the price of one. Sometimes might even get three or four things done up with just one walk out to the back yard.

You know I have used that piece of wisdom a lot throughout my life and I am sure glad he shared it with me.

Also come spring I usually have a pile of sawdust from cutting up firewood laying around and what I like to do is mix it with some good old cow manure or any other compost I might have laying around. I don't usually use it the first year, as sawdust has to have time to break down. Also one has to remember only certain kinds are good for gardens, pine, maple, ash, are a few of my favorites, walnut should never be used as far as I am concerned. Some have had good results using it for a year or so, then problems start to arise with things not growing right, so...... I just stay away from it.

Red and white oak now isn't too bad, but for me to use it, it would have had to be rotting for around three or four years and then mixed real good with some compost. One just has to think ahead a wee bit when it comes to farming, gardening and things, as it can save a person a lot of grief.

Some say gardening can be expensive. I say, well for some I suspect it is. For my wife and I though most of our expense each year is paid back in the fall, by selling a bit of our produce to different folks. But even if we choose not to sell, one can't forget all them healthy preserves that are just waiting to be tasted and not having to be bought in the grocery store. Especially throughout the winter months when things double in price, if not more.

Years ago I bought this one farm, that had a lot of Bartlet Pear trees on it. It had been let go pretty bad, with the trees not being trimmed or no fertilizer, meaning manure, added to the soil for God knows when. Well......took a lot of planning and hard work but in two years the end results was more than I expected.

I did that a lot throughout my life, taking old farms and bringing them back into productivity. Seems that when I came upon a farm that had been just let go, something inside me got to working and one thing would lead to another and in a few years I would have them back to the way a farm should be.

The farming world of today has been complicated in my eyes, some have to have the best of everything when it comes to equipment, you name it. The only thing that does, is put a financial strain on ones self, and, they don't do so well.

For myself, all through my farming days, I never ever had a brand new tractor, just didn't seem right for some reason spending all that money. I always figured there was plenty of good old used ones out there, that with a wee bit of work would do the same job as a new one. Did that with a lot of things thinking back.

So to sum things up and don't get me wrong, I do feel very badly the way things have gone with farming over the years, and, a lot of folks are sorry about it, but as my old Dad always said.

"Being sorry doesn't get things done, it sounds good, but that's as far as it goes."

A Few Words of Wisdom From My Friend Grey Wolf...

Inside each of us is a voice. It is a quiet voice. It is a guiding voice. If we listen for it, it will guide us, and help us avoid disaster. It is especially active when we are afraid, when we are in doubt, when we are scared, when we need help, and when we get angry.

If we are excited emotionally, it is hard to hear this voice. If we are angry, it's hard to hear this voice because it is usually quiet. The best thing we can do is to practice getting quiet. If we don't get quiet, there is another voice called the judge. It tells us to attack or say bad things to other people or to judge ourselves. This voice is loud and usually gets us into trouble.

Living In The Past

You know some say living in the past is a bad thing, get on with today and that's that. I for one don't agree with that saying, as over the years many a good thing has come about by living out some of the ways of past tense.

For example, like cutting and splitting wood. Remembering back, one year I ordered some wood from some folks, logs to be exact and had them piled by my house here. Been awhile since I cut wood to this extent, but figured it would help out by saving us a bit of money. Well once into cutting and splitting it, one finds that he has muscles where he didn't know he had them. But after a day or so the old body adapted and things got a bit easier.

I was having a bit of a time splitting my wood at first, as I bought a new splitting Axe and well, giving it some thought I remembered years ago what old Reg, the feller that raised me used to say.

"George never use a sharp Axe to split wood on a day with temperatures below freezing. Reason being, a sharp Axe gets stuck in the wood, where a dull Axe doesn't, as when the Axe strikes the wood being a wee bit on the dull side, it tends to bounce a bit. But what it is really doing, it's making a sort of dent and pushing the wood down into the dent. A couple times doing that and you will notice a crack forming, and, well, the rest is a piece of cake.

Now comes the gas or electric log splitter that folks want you to buy now a days. My son asked if I wanted one, but after giving it some thought I told him to forget it. You know I have found over the years, that as long as it's freezing outside there is no need for a wood splitter. By the time two fellows gets a piece put into place I could have three or four already split by hand. I am not bragging, it's just the way it is and the feeling one gets when a piece splits, well, one just has to have done it.

One old piece of equipment that has been put out to pasture so to speak, is the old Cant-Hook. When it comes to moving logs around this is one piece that can sure make a hard job easier.

In another perspective, growing up on the farm I got to say has helped me more today than anything. All the things that my elders taught me still comes into play each and every day. I can't see any better way to live, than to sit for a bit each day and reflect back on what I was taught. I don't call it living in the past, I call it using the past to live today.

Sure there is lots to be said for today no denying that. Just that for me I have found that a lot of things of today just makes more work for a feller. I know, some of them worked out to my benefit as some did years ago but for most parts just using ones mind has made my life simpler and also puts money back into my pocket. Right way of looking at it? To each their own I suppose would be the best way to answer that.

My wife for example, she wouldn't have a dishwasher, microwave oven, bread maker, electric can opener, fancy stove, electric kettle, well the list goes on and on. She has always said she can do the job better and faster by using the old ways. Watching and living with her for over thirty some years one soon learns she is telling the truth.

Got to talking to a fellow one time and he asked how we made out being so far away from the cities when it comes to buying things like food or hardware. I told him that we had them things right here in town if we needed them. Also I told him that like years ago most country folks and I mean country folks, hardly ever went to town, as we grew our own. In my mind it's on the plus side living a good distance from the big cities, as you learn to live with what you got and not what you want.

Not saying now that there is anything wrong with city life, as I am not. Why should I, heck I have two boys that live in the city and love it. Different folks like different things that's all, simple as that.

Yep life was hard back when and still isn't the easiest today. For example today my mind says I can still do things that I did when I was twenty. Only problem is when I get to doing some of them my body says, hold up there a might and rightly so too.

You know I think if I was to single out any bit of wisdom that I have learned, that has helped me the most, it would be knowing the difference between, needing and wanting. When asked what I would do, if I had to do it all over again?

"I wouldn't change one thing, as every obstacle or incident that has been put in front of me, has gotten me to where I am today, and that is enjoying life to the fullest, with the love of my life. Can't ask for anything more than that, can ya?

Peaches

Y ou know years ago on our farm, we had acres of different kinds of peaches. A few kinds of peaches that we grew back then would be. Early Red Haven and Red Haven, Red Skins, Sun Haven, Vanity, and the last peach for the season was Loring. Now most all of these peaches back then were freestone peaches, meaning the pit or stone falls out pretty well on their own, when you slice one in half. The freestones are also the easiest to work with when it comes to preserving. The cling-stone peaches were also nice, but more work was involved and over the years folks kind of got away from them.

My favorite peach the Elberta is not grown much anymore. It was about the nicest peach one could ever get for canning or just eating out of your hand. The flesh was a deep yellow and so juicy it would run down your face while eating. It was sweet but yet tart tasting and when you bit into it you knew you had something. But like a lot of fruits, they were replaced with different varieties. One reason being they had to be handled with care when picking and trucking to market as they bruised easily.

After they were phased out we started growing Loring, now they were a peach, almost the same as the Elberta's, a freestone and folks just gobbled them up. I always remember on the market folks would ask me what Freestone meant. I always told them.

"I don't charge for the pit."

Satisfied a lot of folks just saying that and got a laugh or two at the same time, but as I said earlier a freestone peach is when the flesh falls away from the stone after cutting it open. An easy way to find out if you have a good freestone, is just take the peach in your hands and give it a easy twist. If it is it will break right in half easily and the pit will fall out on the floor. I don't know how many thousands of baskets we sold over the years, but I do know this, I enjoyed each and ever day of growing them.

Peaches or any fruit today, like apples and pears should be pealed before eating anymore because of all the pesticides they are using. Don't think you can get away by washing the fruit either, I know they tell you to wash them before eating as with anything but in reality, one would have a hard time getting the sprays off the fruit. Reason being is when the farmers spray today they put the pesticides in the sprayer, they then mix in stickers. Stickers is something you probably don't even know about unless you are a farmer or in the business of fruit farming. What is it? Well stickers is what they mix in with the water and pesticides or fungicides, this holds the pesticides and things on the fruit so they can't be easily wash off in the rain. So it doesn't take a scientist to tell you that washing your fruit under a tap doesn't help much, so I recommend that you peel them when at all possible. Darn shame too as a lot of the goodness one needs is in the peel.

The best way to beat the system is to go and buy yourself a couple peach trees of your own and get them growing. That's a sure fire way of beating all the pesticides and enjoying the true flavor of a peach. I don't really know why folks don't do more of that as some spend thousands of dollars on all kinds of trees for their back yards, that doesn't do anything, other than nice to look at or sit under. My way of thinking is, put in different fruit trees instead and you then get the best of all worlds.

I would also like to say here a few words on growing peaches without using pesticides. I have found that by planting flowering broad leaf plants in peach orchards that they become more attractive hosts for all kinds of insects and when this happens, the peaches are left alone. When that happens, one can then in turn, reduce the need for insecticides throughout the growing season. Also planting garlic near peach trees reduces the risk of peach leaf curl, a common disease.

Final note for planting peaches, one tree is all you need in the home garden, because they are self-pollinating, but at least two pear trees of different kinds must be planted together to ensure successful cross-pollination and fruit set. Bosc and Bartlett pears are ideal companions for pollination and to top it off, they love to grow near peach trees.

Well there you have it, a bit on peaches, old and new. In saying that I hope it gets some folks inspired enough to get out there and plant a tree or two. I do know this, what could be better than to be sitting out under a nice peach, pear or apple tree on them warm summer days and be able to just reach up and grab a nice juicy peach without moving, now that is living in my eyes.

Figured with all the talk on peaches I would let you know how we do them up for winter. Years ago we used to put them in jars, which was good. Today though my wife and I have found we like them better frozen. Just seems to taste better for some reason. Here is how my lovely wife does it.

Freezing Peaches

First slice the peaches and put them in a large bowl. Then sprinkle with Fruit Fresh according to directions on the jar. Mix gently and put in ziploc bags, or plastic containers. Once done, freeze, that's all there is to it. The Fruit Fresh is just a vitamin C powder that keeps them from turning dark. You can make a syrup and freeze them in it if you like, but is not necessary. Also, you can freeze with sugar, but it's up to you. If you freeze without sugar, you can defrost and make jam later on. Can't beat that huh? Enjoy!

Final Note: Eating lots of fruits, vegetables, seeds, nuts, and grains helps open the door to your storehouse of memories. In other words, they help you achieve success in every area, throughout your life.

Tomatoes

On the farm come summer, tomatoes was our biggest concern. The thing about crops on a farm is that there is a certain time that things have to be done. Even today here where we live now, I find myself out in the vegetable garden doing the same as I did years ago on the farm.

For example, come mid summer, tomatoes should be hilled up as one would do with potatoes and cucumbers and for three generations our family has done this with great success.

In the spring I try and keep all my grass cuttings and let it rot at one end of the garden, then come those hot days of summer I spread it around the base of the plants. This not only gives the plants the boost they need but also kills off a lot of weeds that might arise. Once the rotten grass is put down, I let it sit for a day or so, I then start working up the soil and grass cuttings in between the rows. I just walk along with a hoe and pull the earth up to the plants on one side, then back down the other. In doing this one also cuts off the weeds and covers them up which in return also acts as fertilizer for the plants. Only takes a bit of time to hill them and the rewards are too many to count.

Folks ask if I stake my tomatoes, and I just tell them I plant them a bit closer together, which allows them to lean on each other, which holds them up. In reality that is actually what happens, as between the hilling and the planting a bit close, they don't fall over as much. If one thinks about it, how would one stake say fifty acres of them, just wouldn't be heard of. Usually on our farm they were just let be and we never had a problem. Sure you loose a few here and there, but that's to be expected with such a large acreage.

Today of course I have downsized a lot since selling the farms, but I still put in around 75 tomato plants, for our own use and maybe a few to sell here and there if the year permits.

If frost was a problem back on the farm we dealt with it a bit different than I do here now. What we would do would be to soak the ground with water the night before and most of the time that would save the crop. That remedy works great for a couple nights as the moisture comes up from the warm damp ground and keeps the frost off the plants. But if the weather stays cold for more than a couple days other problems arise, as you can be plagued with disease. Joys of being a farmer.

Thing one should not do though, is if, lets say, it rained the day before the frost is called for. If one would have put plastic down with the ground being wet, it would have made the problem worse. Only time to cover the plants is if the ground is dry. Old time wisdom pays off again.

Some folks like to sucker their plants and I suppose it helps to some extent in producing larger tomatoes. I kind of figure it this way though, old Mother Nature has been around for years and them suckers are put there for a reason. They shade the ground and allow the moisture not to be dried up as easily throughout them hot summer days. In the long run you get real nice healthy plants with lots of tomatoes. Maybe a touch smaller, but I have found that the smaller tomatoes have the best taste for canning and sandwiches and isn't that what we are looking for?

Now in saying this, every once in awhile a year will come along that is really wet. When that happens I would recommend you sucker your plants, as it will then allow the soil to dry out a bit and stop a lot of rotting. How to sucker the plants is as I mentioned in an earlier story, but worth mentioning again.

When looking at a tomato plant you will see the arms striking off from the main plant. Now look under the arm and you will see one pointing down toward the ground. These are suckers, they produce nothing. So just push them in a downward motion and they will break off very easily, that's all there is to it.

Tomatoes have a wealth of health benefits for folks, just too many to name and new things being found out each day too. Same as earth, yep good old dirt, lots of folks think that earth is bad for you, but in reality earth is good, as most things we eat comes from it.

I remember years ago when I was brought into the house for supper, being a young feller, my mouth was covered with dirt. Reason being everything that a young fellow or gal plays with or handles, goes into the mouth. Didn't hurt us one bit, and my thinking it kind of helped us, as our systems became used to these things and then was capable of fighting off diseases.

Myself I love to take a hand full of fresh worked soil and just smell it. The smell that it gives off is something I can't get enough of, especially in the spring. Give it a try, I am sure you will be pleasantly surprised. I know it sounds kind of silly to some I suppose, but not to me.

Tomatoes also like growing next to other vegetables and things and here are a few; Asparagus, Basil, Bush Beans, Cabbage, Carrots, Celery, Marigolds, Mint, Onions, Parsley and Peppers. They don't like growing near; Corn, Dill, Fennel, Pole Beans or Potatoes.

One meal that I would recommend for folks that will help immensley with all types of diseases and cancer would be this. It consisted of mashed sweet potatoes, with a salad of finely chopped raw broccoli and tomatoes (the two key ingredients) Brussels sprouts, cucumber, and olive oil, that's it and your body will love you for it. The amount of tomatoes and broccoli is approximately
1 1/4 cups of raw broccoli and 2 1/2 cups of fresh tomatoes to create the anti-cancer super food combo. What have you got to loose?

Well there you go, a bit more on tomatoes. Hope you all get out there now and hill them up, and when the hot weather hits, they will thank you for it with rewards in numbers.

A couple quick things. Tomatoes love sun, hot weather and water, and for those that don't grow their own, don't forget to support your local farmers market, without your support they will parish completely.

Our Home Made Tomato Soup Recipe

2 tbsp. extra virgin olive oil
1 medium onion, chopped
1-2 cloves garlic, chopped
1 medium carrot, chopped into small pieces
1 stalk celery with leaves, chopped into small pieces
3-4 cups chopped tomatoes (1&1/2 pounds)
1 tbsp. flour
3 cups water
1-2 tbsp. fresh basil
1 teaspoon salt

Lightly cook the garlic, onion and carrots, then mix everything together. Bring to boil, then simmer for 20 – 30 minutes. Now the only thing missing is a few slices of home made bread fresh out of the oven. So..... good. Enjoy!

Potato Growing

Years ago just down the road from us, lived an old feller that grew potatoes. He was a nice fellow and no matter what time of the day one dropped by, he would always take a few minutes to sit and chat. I have to say he grew the best tasting potatoes one has ever eaten.

I always remember Laura would get me to go and get some of the wee little ones, when they first started digging. She would then wash them and spread them around a roast of beef and let them simmer in the juices most the afternoon and come supper, well you were in for a tasty meal that's for sure.

Thinking about that got me to remembering how I went about growing them and figured I would put down a few words here on the subject.

Growing potatoes don't take a great amount of work, but they do require a bit of care, meaning the preparation of getting the soil ready. One thing potatoes like is sandy loam with a few rocks thrown in for drainage. I was taught, one could tell the type of land just by taking a hand full of dirt and squeezing it.

If the dirt sticks together in a ball, one usually has a bit of clay in it, or all clay. If it comes apart slightly after squeezing it and kind of runs out of your hand, you have some nice loam, and finally if it runs right out of your hand after squeezing it you probably have sandy soil.

Here in the north most of us have got good earth with a bit of sand thrown in, which is a good thing. Only thing on the down side is that it drys out a bit fast, but if one has a good water source and keeps putting compost in the soil every year, he or she is all set. Here on our property we have two wells, a drilled and a dug. The dug well we use for watering our garden, but if it gets real dry it pretty well dries up and we then have to use our drilled well. I also have a couple rain barrels setting under the eve troughs catching the rain water, as no use in letting it go to waste. No better water on earth for plants, than fresh rain water, good for your house plants too.

What I do is start off digging a trench for whatever length you decide on, about a foot deep. At the bottom of the trench I loosen the dirt a bit more and bring the loose dirt up about six inches, I then get to placing my seed potatoes all in row, around six inches apart. One thing I should say here is that if possible don't plant potatoes purchased from the grocery store — they are not reliable for use as seed potatoes because they have been sprayed to retard sprouting and if one goes to all the work of planting them, we want to have the best crop one can get, right? I always figure one can have enough problems doing things right, so why add to it.

Once you have grown your own potatoes though you can save a few for the next growing season as one usually has a basket or two left over.

After they get growing, if you see tube like runners along the ground, that means you haven't hilled them up properly, so get your hoe out of the shed and start hilling them with soil, just pull it up about three inches or so around the bottoms.

Planting time around our home would be around the first or second week of May, as they are under ground and the frost won't hurt them. Not too early though as if the ground isn't warm they won't do much anyways. You could also put in two crops, one first thing in the spring and one a month later, that way you will have some fresh potatoes for fall, which is what we do.

Once the tops start to turn brown near the end of summer you are ready to enjoy all that this old earth has given you. Remember if they are green color when digging them up come harvest time I don't recommend you eating them. Reason that some are green on top is that the sun has gotten to them because you didn't cover them well enough when hilling. Not a big deal though as I am sure you will find lots of nice ones a bit deeper down when you get to digging.

Friends of Potatoes are; Beans, Cabbage, Corn, Eggplant, Horseradish, Lettuce, Marigolds, Petunias, Onions and Peas.

They don't like being near; Melons, Parsnips, Rutabagas, Squash, Sunflowers, Tomatoes and Turnips.

Another reason for eating home grown pesticide free potatoes, is that they contain tryptophan, and eaten at supper will for sure help you in getting a good nights sleep. I would also like to mention here that within eight to 36 hours after switching to organic fruit and vegitables, studies have shown that the pesticides in ones body almost disappeared completely. Just another reason to seek out good organic fruit and vegetables, or better yet get outside and start your own garden, don't you think?

A nice thing to try is just to take a few potatoes fresh from the garden and boil them up, just till they are soft, don't over cook them. Take these straight from the pot and eat with nothing added, you are in for a treat. One thing about growing your own, you know what you got. I keep on saying that I know, but I figure it's worth mentioning as here in the north, we have some of the best darn soil on the planet, so why not put it to good use. There is nothing better than front porch sittin', watching your supper growing at your feet. Wouldn't you agree?

Now here is another old time treat straight from Laura's old cook book, called, Potato Cake, you gotta try it.

Potato Cake

Boil, cool then crush cold potatoes with butter and salt. Mix in a small portion of flour and a little yeast, (the last may be omitted at pleasure.) Then with milk work the whole to a constancy of very firm dough. Now roll it out to a thickness of 1½" - 2". Cut it out the size of your frying pan, previously greased and lay in your cake, after flouring it all over. Bake covered with a plate, shake and shift it from time to time to prevent burning. When half done turn it and cover with a plate once again.

That's it, cook to taste and put it on your plate. For mine, as soon as it comes out of the frying pan I like to add one spoon full of real butter directly to the top, with just a touch of sea salt. I gotta tell ya, it's mouth watering good. Enjoy!

Potato/Wild Onion Soup (makes about 7 cups)

It's easy to make, has a great texture and is absolutely delicious. Especially good in cold weather.
5 medium potatoes, peeled
1 bunch of green onions (wild or domestic), or 2 leeks chopped in pieces, not to finely.
6 cups water
1 tsp. sea salt, or to taste.
Simmer all together until the potatoes crumble under pressure.
Add 1/8 tsp. pepper, or to taste.

It also freezes well, so make a bunch. Some people like to add milk, cream or butter. You can also add cooked clams, carrots & corn to make a chowder.
That's it and so...... good for ya.

Lessons Well Learned

Lessons in today's world are something that in my eyes needs to be looked at, when it comes to our young ones. If you would ask my lovely wife about raising young ones, she would tell you very directly that we protect them too much for their own good, my feelings completely.

In saying this, one story comes to mind from years ago, well there might be a few, but for now.

It was summer time thinking back, Dad had been out in the fields planting and had just walked up to the barn where I was sitting. Out near the barn was a vegetable garden and throughout it, was six or so rows of real nice red peppers. Well I got to looking at them things and being near the end of the afternoon I was getting a bit hungry. Dad walked over to see me and said.

"Lets go to the well and get us a cool glass of water, it sure is a hot one." I knew he was happy by the sound of his voice so I decided on asking him if I could have one of those nice red peppers to eat.

"I told you George, they are not for eating, how many times do I have to tell you?"

"But Dad, it's not that you don't have enough of them, darn you have rows of the things, you wouldn't miss one would ya?"

Well after a bit of persuading on my part he finally sat down by the well and said.

"Well there young feller, I told you I don't think you should, but....... if you got a hankering to have one, I won't stand in your way."

With that I took off on the run over to the garden and picked the biggest reddest one I could find. I then took it back and sat down beside my Dad. Boy I thought, this is going to be the best ever, as I have been waiting for this day for a month now. I looked at Dad and again he said.

"Your decision, you know what I think."

With that I took the biggest bite I could get into my mouth. For about one minute things went real good. The sweet taste of the pepper filled my mouth, that made my taste buds almost jump out and onto the ground. Then it happened, from sweet and juicy, to hot and then hotter and after that even hotter. I grabbed the old tin cup hanging on the pump and went to get a drink of water to cool things down and in doing so Dad grabbed my arm.

"I wouldn't do that if I were you, he said."

"Well I am not you I hollered and pumped myself a nice drink of cool water.

"Suit yourself," he said, "but don't say I didn't warn ya."

In my mind I couldn't wait to get this cold water into my burning mouth, but what happened next was almost unbearable. As soon as the cold water hit my mouth it seemed to stop the burning, but then to my surprise, I found it made it worse, a lot worse. I got up with tears in my eyes and said.

"You knew this was going to happen didn't you?"

"Yep I did," he said.

"Well why didn't you tell me?"

"Well, I told you not to eat one, but you didn't listen, you kept pestering at me to have one. Now you know that if old Dad says you shouldn't do or eat something, that he is tellin' you for your own good."

"Well, ya, but sheesh Dad, you could have explained the reason behind why I shouldn't eat one of them peppers."

"Would that really have mattered?" he asked.

"Well not likely." "Guess I had to learn on my own."

"Yep, that's what I figured too, now just give it about ten minutes and that cool water will be pretty tasty."

"Sounds good, and you know Dad, I think from now on I will stick to apples, peaches, pears or something that I know."

"Good idea son, good idea."

With that we went and laid down under a tree for a bit and I listened to one of his learning experiences when he was a boy.

One Special Weed

One day years ago on the dairy farm I remember Reg saying.

"Well George we have a problem that needs attending in number three field."

Reg had numbered the fields years before so if Laura the lady of the house needed us, she would know where we were at.

I pulled my chair up to the table and asked what the problem was, as Reg usually never acknowledged a problem, let alone admit he had a problem.

"Well he said, for the past few years I have been using that number three field for pasture, but lately I have been noticing it growing a lot of old bull thistles. Once they get to growing on a man's land you can bet your last dollar that problems are in the works, unless we get to them before they take hold. The first thing in dealing with them sons-a-guns, is getting us both a good pair of leather gloves, as they sure can make a mess of a fellers hands.

"I have just the thing, said Laura I made three pair last winter out of the deer hides that was left over from the horse blankets I made."

"Woman after my own heart there George, you will be a lucky man to land one like that in your day."

"Hush now," said Laura, "don't be talking women to a boy of his age."

Reg smiled and said. "Come on boy, lets you and me head on out to the tool shed and get the scythe out as that is what is going to be needed first."

72

With that, Laura spoke up and said, "you two take care now, I don't want to be having to dig out barbs from them thistles all evening and if you both are real good, I will bring out a couple pieces of pie around ten and a cool drink of water."

That sure put a smile on both our faces.

Once we got to the field Reg started right in at cutting the thistles.

"I got to say there is sure a mess of them Reg. How long do you figure it will it take to get them all cut down"

"Well there is roughly an acre here, so I figure if you stop talking and get putting them in piles as I cut them, we should be done in a few days. Once it drys we will then set a match to it. Only way a fellow can get rid of them once and for all. All that blue you see out there, is full of seeds, and I'll tell ya, if a big wind comes up, well that would mean thousands more."

We both then went to work and sure enough a few days later it was cleared, but it didn't get done without a lot of sweat, as mid week we had a scorcher of a hot spell. Reg and I were just soaked with sweat and at the end of each day the both of us were all in. Laura though kept us refreshed with cool water along with friendly smiles and a hug now and then that made the hot days go by quicker.

Once done I remember Laura saying. "I have been giving it some thought and with you two working so hard in cutting them darn thistles, that tonight after supper we are going to have ourselves a bit of a good time and touch a match to them piles."

And thats exactly what we did. We invited a few folks from up the road aways as that's the way things were done back then.

After the chores were done we all headed on out to the field, we found a couple old logs and Reg pulled them into place. Once we were all settled I was told to lite up the piles which I did. We then all took to singing and for the next few hours we had ourselves a good old time. Hot dogs were roasted in between songs and a ice cold home made punch was served to wash it all down.

"Pretty rough life huh?" I asked Reg.

"Sure is George, sure is."

A couple days later Reg hooked up the Clyde's to the plow, saying. "Just cutting the tops was only part of it, as them roots given a chance would bring upon us a whole mess more work."

Took a day or so for Reg to get it all plowed and while he did that Laura and me picked up all the roots we could find and put them in a pile. I didn't mind, as I knew we were in for another evening of fun, when all said and done.

Some of the roots though, Laura cooked up for meals and other parts she dried for mixing in with stews and soups, saying it was real good for us.

Yep some days were hard back then, but you know, we never let them days get the best of us. How? Well when a hard one came upon us, we did

73

our very best to make it into something good. Looking back I thought I hated them old bull thistles, but today I realize they were a friend, as they brought our family, a wee bit closer together.

My good friend Grey Wolf always said: "Man is the only critter who feels the need to label things as flowers or weeds."

Remember this, where bull thistles grow, good soil lays beneath and here is something I put together, a scale of what the pH in soil should be for a few vegetables.

pH Scale

Asparagus, 6.0-8.0
Bean, pole, 6.0-7.5
Beet, 6.0-7.5
Broccoli, 6.0-7.0
Brussels sprout, 6.0-7.5
Carrot, 5.5-7.0
Cauliflower, 5.5-7.5
Celery, 5.8-7.0
Chive, 6.0-7.0
Cucumber, 5.5-7.0
Garlic, 5.5-8.0
Lettuce, 6.0-7.0
Pea, sweet, 6.0-7.5
Pepper, sweet, 5.5-7.0
Potato, 4.8-6.5
Pumpkin,5.5-7.5
Radish, 6.0-7.0
Spinach, 6.0-7.5
Squash, 6.0-7.5
Tomato, 5.5-7.5

Old Time Remedy

Over the years here in Canada and the United States we have had remedies for our health, that I feel has slipped through the cracks. I would never say that the old time remedies are a reason for not seeing your doctor though if something should need attention. But there is a lot of things out there that is readily available to folks if they just knew where to look. The old saying is and I really believe this, is that there is never a problem or disease that somewhere right beside it is a fix or remedy. One of those old time remedies is readily available here in the north, along with most of Canada and the U.S.A. It comes from the Basswood Tree.

Thinking back when my Grandfather was alive, he would tell of how the Basswood tree or some call it the Linden tree, has the potential of helping those suffering from a cold or flu. How it works is that every so often the tree comes out in blossom and that's the time to start stocking up. The tree doesn't blossom every year and to me it seems that it has a mind of its own.

Out back of our house we had a huge one until a bad storm came through one summer and uprooted it, was like loosing a good friend. The first year we moved here it didn't blossom, but the next it was loaded. The time to pick the blossoms is when they are out in full bloom. There will be no problem knowing when the time is right, or for that matter if there is a tree close by, as the scent it throws off can be smelt for miles. A real sweet aroma will fill the air and linger there for days. The actual reason the tree does this, is to attract the bees for pollination, but it's a good signal that this is the time for us humans to get stocked up with a cold remedy.

75

When you do find the tree, the things to look for are these. When looking at the tree you will see the large basswood leaves, they are not what you want. When the blossoms come out in full bloom there will be clusters of them and just below the clusters, there is two or three long narrow leaves. The blossoms and the long narrow leaf is what you want to pick. I picked a half bushel from my tree the last time they came into bloom.

You then take the blossom cluster's and long narrow leaf, which by the way will pretty well come off together, and you put them somewhere that you can spread them out to dry for a month or so. Every once in awhile move them around so that the air can get all around them and they dry real good. Don't need them getting moldy or rotting as that would be like throwing away a thousand dollar bill.

Once that is done, then put them in a brown paper bag, you know, the ones like you use to take your lunch in when going to school. Not sure if they still do that, been awhile for me.

Anyways, once all dried and put away, along comes winter and even though I faithfully wash my hands after being out, occasionally a cold grabs me or tries. When that happens and I feel myself coming down with one, my lovely wife gets out the blossoms and with her hand just crunches up a few with one leaf. The leaves promote a bit of warmth and breaks up a fever, the blossoms are the cure. She puts, oh...... about two tablespoons into a loose tea holder, you can buy them pretty well anywhere. In doing that she then lets it hang in a cup of hot boiled water. After five minutes you have a real tasty drink and your on the way to recovery. Oh, you can add a touch of honey or sugar for taste if you so choose.

I have used this remedy for years, as my Grandfather and Dad before me. Works great and in no time you are back to your old self. The only down side is, you might not get that sick day off work.

Now lets say you left some blossoms on the tree and let them go through their stages, what you would end up with then, would be a nut like fruit. The fruit or nut isn't too good for a cold anymore, but if you grind them up and mix a wee bit of sugar, you will find it makes for a real nice chocolate drink. Over in Germany the kids have been drinking it for years and can't get enough of it.

So the next time you catch the sweet smell of the old Basswood tree, head on out and see if you can find it, you won't be disappointed. Then at the first signs of a cold or flu, open that brown bag and make yourself a nice hot tea from the blossoms, sit back and let nature take its course.

The only other advice I can give you for a cold remedy, is not a remedy, it's preventative medicine, never touch your face with your hands, make it a habit and as soon as you get home from being out, give them a quick wash.

So no excuse now, when summer arrives, keep your nose to the air for the Basswood blossoms, and when I go to town, I don't want to see or hear any honking or sniffing.

Real Butter

Another thing that I really enjoyed eating years ago, was home made butter that Laura made for our meals. I got to tell ya, it is a taste that, well you would have to try it to really get the full meaning. In plain language, it was darn good and kept you coming back for more.

The way we made it back then wasn't without a bit of work, but the finished product was sure worth the effort and besides, we couldn't afford to buy store boughten butter.

We would start off with the milking of the cows in the morning as that was the best time, evenings we were all too tired to do anything other than maybe a bit of reading. Once the milking was done we would take the milk and put it in the separator, which was a machine that separated the cream from the milk. Not a powered one either, as the only power we had back then was hand power. Once that was done the cream would be brought into the house and dumped into an old wooden churn. Worked slick too and one really could do it today if he or she had one. I have been giving some thought on making one, as they are not too complicated, just got to find or make the time.

As soon as the cream is poured into the churn, one would then pull it up and down with a rod that ran down the center of it. It had a paddle hooked on one end and it just churned the cream up and down till the butter separated again from the milk. The separator did most the work but there was still some milk mixed in and the churning took care of that in a short time.

Once that was done, Laura would take the butter which had separated from the milk and mix them together with a bit of water and the remainder of the milk would go one way and the butter the other. It was then put back in the churn and you would work it a bit more. Once that was done, you then had butter.

It was then taken from the churn and she would put it in containers she had from years past and stored in the cold room, job done other than enjoying it and we sure did that.

I also remember when Laura made the butter that, once in awhile in the winter it wouldn't have the same yellow color to it and one day I asked her about it.

"Well she said, the reason for that is, it was cooler in the house when we made it and the butter looses its color when cold. What I do then is, when the churning is about half done, I take a hot poker from the stove and dunk it into the butter and doing so warms up the cream which brings back a bit of color.

Sometimes if a lot of color is lost, I take some juice from the carrots and mix that in with the butter and there you go, colored butter. Once in awhile though I don't put enough in and you don't get the same look, but other than that it still tastes good."

Yep life was good back then and them kind of things today make me yearn for the days of past years.

Final note, I think we would all have a lot to gain, if we just took, at the very least, a quick look at how our Elders lived, so many years ago.

Recipe For
Waffles Made With Real Butter

One quart of sweet or sour milk.
Four eggs.
Two-thirds of a cup of real butter.
Half a teaspoon of salt.
Three teaspoons of baking powder.
Flower enough to make a nice batter.
If you use sour milk leave out the baking powder and use two teaspoons of baking soda.

Only thing missing now is some home made maple syrup. Enjoy!

A few recent studies on the benefits of real butter

The idea of margarine was sold to physicians much like drugs are sold today. Some physicians told their patients to stop eating butter and start eating margarine.
Soon everyone 'knew' that margarine was better for health than butter.

Once an idea becomes popular opinion though, it tends to persist even in the face of evidence to the contrary. Today, butter is still viewed as our enemy in spite of the fact that hundreds of highly motivated studies have been unable to confirm a link between butter and disease.

Does butter really cause disease? Quite the contrary. Butter actually protects us against many of the diseases on the increase today. Here are a few things to look at.

1---- Butter is an agent of weight loss, not weight gain.

2---- Butter is one of the few foods that supply an adequate amount of iodine in a highly absorbent form. Iodine is critical for proper thyroid functioning as is vitamin A.

3---- The fat soluble antioxidant vitamins in butter as well as selenium and cholesterol, are also protective against cancer.

4---- And what about cholesterol, that nasty substance the medical industry says is out to get us? Cholesterol is actually necessary for proper cell functioning and is a powerful antioxidant that protects us from damaged and rancid fats, such as those generated by highly processed vegetable oils. Butter is an important source of this vital nutrient.

5---- Although heart disease was seldom seen a hundred years ago, today it is the number one killer. During this time period, the annual consumption of butter has decreases from eighteen pounds per person to less than four. Butter is rich in nutrients that protect the heart. Also one should note that among the beneficial nutrients in butter is the antioxidant, vitamin A, needed for health of the thyroid and adrenal glands which help maintain proper functioning of the whole cardiovascular system. Butter is the best and most readily absorbed source of vitamin A. Butter also contains lecithin, a substance needed for the proper assimilation and metabolism of cholesterol and other fat constituents. It also contains the antioxidant vitamin E and selenium which are protective of the whole cardiovascular system.
So kind of makes a person think of how he or she should be looking at things, don't ya think?

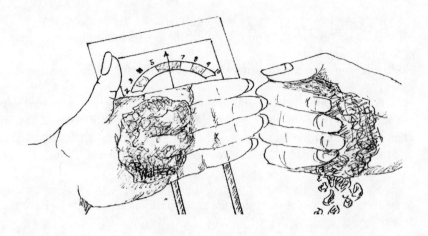

Soil

Y ou know in my books one can't get any more wholesome, fresh, chemical free vegetables, than if they grew their own. It doesn't take as much land either, as some would think to grow a few things. Most folks I would think could spare a wee spot around their property, even if they changed their design of flower gardens. For years I have told folks about utilizing the space that they do have, introducing produce that not only looks good, but things that you can eat and enjoy all season long. Even folks that live in apartments with balcony's can grow their own vegetables, as all they would need is a few pots to get them started.

There is nothing nicer in my books than to let good soil run through ones hands on a warm summers day. Just to pick up a hand-full and smell the aroma it throws off and how it feels is something that most folks just take for granted. I know folks just think it's dirt and dirt gets you dirty, and one can get sick if they touch it. Well that's wrong, or at least to my thinking.

As I said in other stories, years ago when any one or two year old came in the house, you just had to look at their face to know what they were eating, yep good old dirt. Thing is, if one really looked at soil they would probably find enough bad things in it to kill a horse.

But how come it doesn't or didn't bother humans, well reason being we use to allow our young ones to be subjected to these so called bad things and over the years they built up immunities to them. Now a days we protect our young ones so much, not saying that is a bad thing, but in my eyes I think we are over doing it a mite.

I myself can't get enough of the good old soil throughout the summer months, my old Dad said it was in my genes and the name George means tiller of soil. Never really thought of it that much, but kind of think today that he might have been right in his thinking.

There is all types of soil, rocky, sandy, black loam, clay, you name it we got it here on this old earth and over the years I think I have worked with the most of them. In saying that, the one thing that stands out is, that most all soils are workable, even clay.

Years ago we bought this one piece of land that was, well I would say unfit for growing anything, but my old Dad being the man he was, never let things like that get the better of him.

"Plant things that like the soil," he would always say, and that is what we did. Grapes is what we planted for the first few years on that piece of ground, working in different manures and things. In no time it grew anything we decided to plant, just took a bit of thinking and some hard work. Years later we ended up with a hundred acres of prime farm land.

Yep I think back sometimes of how we did things, not easy by no means but you know it was a good time in life, interesting you might say and what more could a feller ask for.

I remember years ago while working the fields around dinner time, I would get off the old tractor to have my lunch. Most times I would just sit down on the fresh worked soil under a pear or peach tree to eat. I got to tell ya just the smell of the unspoiled soil and the way it looked when turned over on a warm summers day, sure put a special feeling in this old fellers heart.

But times are changing. My way of looking at it today agricultural practices are stripping the soil of all the good things that is needed for us humans to survive. They are taking away all the nutritional value of crops, making unbelievable changes at an alarming rate. For example, Vitamin A has decreased from 41 to 100% in apples, broccoli, onions, potatoes and tomatoes. Both the onions and potatoes saw a 100% loss of Vitamin A, in my lifetime alone.

If you are eating tomatoes for example or produce grown in nutritionally depleted soils, then you are consuming produce that isn't in reality giving your body what it needs, which is pretty well what is happening today with all vegetables we are eating.

Here's a common question about minerals and produce. How do tomatoes or other plants know which minerals to absorb? The answer is that each plant soaks up different minerals. A tomato will take in a certain number of minerals (around 56), and it will absorb no more. It will only take in the 56 that it's intended to do. Sweet potatoes, take in more minerals than regular potatoes, where other plants take in 20 or 30 minerals. So you see, each plant is different in doing what it does. Of course, it can only take in what is available in the soil. So even though a tomato should contain 56 minerals, you may be eating a tomato bought at a grocery store that only contains 12 or 7 minerals.

What does this all mean? Well mineral deficiency subjects us to more diseases, aging, sickness and destruction of our physical well-being than any other factor in personal health. A great many known aliments are directly linked to mineral deficiency, like osteoporosis, heart disease, arthritis, diabetes, liver disease, birth defects and impaired mental functions are just a few. Our health and existence here on earth is more dependent on minerals than the amounts of protein, carbohydrates or calories we consume. From vitamins to almost every process in the human body, minerals are indispensable. However, if minerals are not in the soil as I said before, they can't be in the food. If they're not in the food....they can't be in you! No amount of human made fertilizer, water or cultivation can change that! I hate to say this, but as bad as things look today in terms of minerals in your produce, it's only going to get worse in the foreseeable future, that is if us humans don't recognize the problem and do something about it.

As my friend Grey Wolf said one day: "George, everything on earth has a purpose and is designed special. No two things are created the same. Every once in awhile though in our minds, we have a picture of how things is suppose to be, and often what we see is different from what they really are. When this happens, we often want to control how things are, making them act or behave according to our way of looking at things. In reality though, we need to leave things alone, and we have to realize, that the Creator is running things quite smoothly all on his own."

Your New Vegetable Garden

With spring in the air, I was outside working when a feller dropped by, stranger for only a few minutes I always say. We got to talking and after a bit he asked me how to get a vegetable garden growing on ground that hasn't been used in years.

"Don't take too much, other than work," I told him.

To start off in the fall of the year turn it over good with a shovel, dig down as deep as you can and then just leave it there all winter. If fall isn't to your liking, spring would be fine too. Once that is done, if you have any wood ashes dump them all over the top of the ground you just turned over and let it set a few days. This will kill off a lot of bugs and some diseases that is not needed in your garden. Don't worry much about the old grass that was there when you started, as when all said and done you won't find any of it. Once that is all done up nice, get yourself all the leaves laying around the house and dump it over the top of your just dug earth. Now your all set and you can get that tiller out and go to work. I work mine one way then the other, about four times. If your ground is real hard you might have to do it a couple more times. Good way to know you got it ready to plant, is when you can reach down, grab a handful of nice dirt and it sort of runs off your fingers when you let it go. I always finish tilling my garden by tilling it the way I am going to plant. Makes it easier to get my rows straight, as I can just look at the lines in the soil left by my tiller.

I like to boarder my garden with something, no special reason really, just for looks. I used raspberries around the top of one garden of mine and down one side. Then on one corner we put in a herb area, as my wife loves her herbs for cooking and things, also they help with unwanted guests, come harvesting time, meaning insects and things. On the other side I put in my asparagus, which is a permanent crop also. Takes around three years for you to get going with a crop when it comes to asparagus and raspberries I have found but you have to start sometime.

Same with fruit trees, old saying is, first year they rest, second year they start moving and third year, well, you get to enjoy the the fruit of your labor.

Grapes are the same, three years before you get anything worth while. One thing while I am talking about fruit trees, if you do have some old wood ashes, dump them around the base of the trees, not too much, about a half a pail or so. Just let it lay there and come spring work it in a wee bit. What it does is, it helps with stabilizing the worms in your fruit, you might still get a few but I have had years without any and no pesticides needed. I like that.

I also like to take some white latex and paint the bottom of my small trees, say about a foot up in height. This also will discourage any ground insects from getting onto the leaves.

If you have rabbits, or lots of mice, you should put a steel mesh around the bottom of your tree say about a foot or so high. You can also use some plastic, but make sure you put some holes in it for air to get through, or you might kill your tree, not too tight either.

Another thing I like doing, is if I cut a good size limb off any tree, I like to cover the fresh cut, as this stops any diseases from getting in it. You can buy the black tar like stuff, but you can also just use good old Elmer's White Glue, works just as well.

Back to the garden. Now that you have it all worked up and it's spring, you can get on with your planting. Don't be in a hurry, which some like to do, as if the ground isn't up to around 45 or 50 degrees it isn't going to do much anyways. Once it's worked up though, the sun throughout the day will for sure get things going for ya.

Take your time and make sure of what you want to plant. My wife and I plant what we like and a bit extra for friends and family. One thing I should also say, if you plant raspberries in your garden, make sure you don't plant tomatoes too close, as the two of them can give each other a few problems, so best to keep them apart wherever possible.

I also realize that there are a lot of people that live in apartments, who doesn't have a piece of land, but there are some foods, such as herbs, that you can grow in pots on the windowsill. This is not the greatest, but it can get you by. However, if you do have a yard, even a small yard, you can grow something, and the rewards are too many to name. With just a pocketful of seeds, a person can grow enough fresh vegetables to keep them healthy year round, at a very little cost.

Why should I grow my own some say, as the grocery stores are loaded with good looking fruits and vegetables? Well unfortunately, a lot of things about groceries are quite deceiving. For example, I've seen tomatoes sold, attached to a part of the vine, which says "vine-ripened tomatoes." Well, this sounds all good and fine, but, in reality, they are not ripened on the vine at all. They are picked green. Exposing them to ethylene gas ripens them and turns them red when they are ready to be put out on the store shelves. Ethylene gas is used to ripen tomatoes, bananas and other fruits or vegetables, so what it all boils down to is this. What you think you are getting, really you're not, as most fruits and vegetables in the stores today isn't really fresh at all.

A good example would be, say if you bought a peach in the grocery store they usually are as hard as a rock. That's not how peaches are in the real world, fresh off the tree they smell good, taste delicious and are just a touch on the soft side.

So there you have it, a few tips on gardening from an old farmer. Food for thought some might say.

Here are a few veggies I recommend starting inside, if your starting from seed. Don't forget to give yourself time when planting seeds inside, as it will take about six to eight weeks for them to get growing.

Inside

Basil, Eggplant, Broccoli, Leeks, Brussels sprouts, Lettuce, Cabbage, Cauliflower, Parsley, Peppers, Celery, Chives and last Tomatoes.

And here are the names of the vegetables that I plant right from seed directly to my garden.

Outside

Beans, Bush and Pole, Potatoes, Beets, Radishes, Carrots, Spinach, Squash, summer and winter, Corn, Swiss Chard, Cucumbers, Peas, and Turnips.

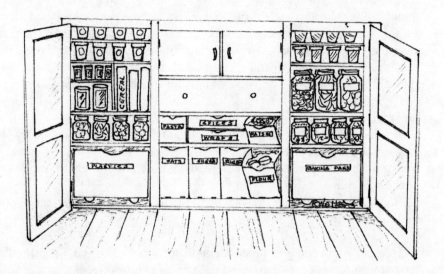

Putting Away For Winter

I gotta' say, living on a farm for most of my life sure has given me a good outlook on things.

Years ago on the Dairy farm Laura the lady of the house would do all kinds of things in getting ready for winter. One of the most important was doing up preserves throughout the summer months, as they came into season. First thing that she done up was jams of all kinds. I can remember going out into the fields where at one special spot grew thousands of wild strawberries. I know one would think it would take you forever to get a basket filled. Not really though, as I could sit in one spot not moving hardly at all and pick a couple quarts or so. Of course I ate as many as I picked, but needless to say it got done.

Later on in the season we got into picking wild blueberries, raspberries, blackberries, red currents and wild goose berries. You can easily find them as they grow in meadows, at river and pond edges, overgrown farm fields, recent places that had a fire, along country roads and lane-ways, and under power line right-of-ways. Another way to find them is to watch nature throughout the year when out for a stroll. I remember Laura one day while we were out walking looked up into a tree and seen a blue jay sitting on a branch. "Look there she said, that old feller is eating a blueberry, must be a patch around close by." We waited a few minutes to see which direction he headed in and followed along, and low and behold we came upon a huge patch just off the trail we were walking on, only a stone throw away.

Once the berries were all done up for the year Laura got into canning things out of the garden, like tomatoes, beets, cucumbers, turnips, you name it, nothing went to waste. Throughout the summer months fields of hay, corn and others were cut and put away in the barn for the critters on them cold winter days. I remember the old barn was just chocked full.

Firewood was high up there on the list of things to get done too, as it was used not only for heat, but all our cooking needs as well. My job was piling it into the woodshed and splitting kindlin', as we used a lot to get the cook stove up to temperature throughout the day.

"Nothing like good dry cedar kindling to get a cook stove oven hot enough to cook pies and things," Laura would always say.

The logs for the firewood were usually cut throughout the winter and left to dry for a year or two. Then we cut and split the logs to size and piled them in the bush to dry even longer. Kind of like an assembly line, where in the end it all came together.

We also had a hog or two and maybe a steer to take to our neighbor as he was a butcher and for a few cords of firewood he would cut and package the meat for us. Great old feller and he not only cut meat, he was also a good Story-Teller too.

I can still hear him saying, "George..... if you don't cut the meat the right way, especially them nice roasts of beef, they will be so tough you could wear out a set of store bought teeth, trying to chew the dang things."

He also said another tip is to hang the meat for a good length of time before you cut it up. I found that to be so true over the years and kind of figure that is why we get so many tough roasts in our stores today.

Also in the fall of the year the old hens quit laying and once that happened we did them up for some Sunday meals, not much went to waste. Laura had a way of taking the feathers from the old chickens, I can't rightly remember how she did it, but she would take the feathers and line Reg's and my leather gloves with them. Boy I have to tell ya, we never had cold hands when old man winter hit.

Once in awhile around the beginning of November, Reg would take me out deer hunting, but that only happened if we didn't do up a steer for meat that year.

Today though my lovely wife and I live here in our country paradise, living about the same as back then. The only difference I guess, would be that we do buy a few more items than years ago, but not much. We kind of fill our needs in life one might say, not our wants.

The nice thing about being self efficient, is that in hard times one is always prepared and I kind of think that is the way it should be. One has to remember, if something major should happen, like a disaster, that the grocery stores would be sold out in hours, not days or weeks.

Wouldn't it be nice to have that bit of security sitting in a pantry?

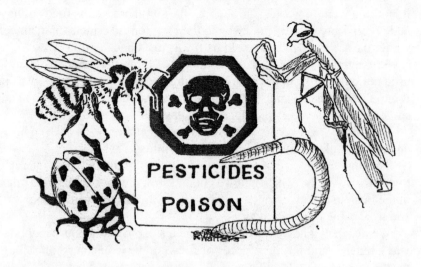

It's Up To You

For years I have written about vegetable gardens and farming, along with stories of my life past and present. The reason for this is to try and get folks outside enjoying nature, along with showing them that all things of years past were not bad. As they most certainly were not.

The health benefits one gets by having a vegetable garden alone would take me a year to put into words if not more. In this story though I would like to talk about a few things, that if not looked at very seriously, could cause us humans a huge amount of grief, to say the least.

The main thing I keep on stressing in some of my stories is we shouldn't be using the pesticides we are using today. I know they tell you they are safe and things like that, but that's their opinion. Mine is, they are wrong. I would bet if blood tests were done on folks today, we would find that most of us are a walking pesticide cocktail.

Think about this, the millions of gallons if not trillions of gallons they spray on lawns, trees, fruit and vegetables, what and where do folks think they go or do. The problem is we are hurting ourselves along with killing off a lot of our good insects like the bees.

You know without the bees this old world would cease to exist. I would say by the time this book comes to press the commercial bee owners would have lost 60 to 70% of their bees already, that is quite frightening. There probably is a lot of things to contribute to this problem but I feel pesticides is one of the biggest on the list.

Along with farming my wife and I also owned and operated a landscaping business. In all the years that we were in business I can honestly say we never sprayed lawns with any pesticides. I proved to my customers that they could have a good looking lawn without using any. For every lawn or garden that is sprayed, there is thousands if not more good insects and bees killed.

The thing is that all a good healthy lawn needs, is fertilizer and water. I have told all my customers that if you happen by a weed in your lawn and don't want it there, bend over and pull it out. If one did that with every walk around his or her lawn, in a short time they wouldn't have any. Simple and a chemical free way of doing things.

Even all the years we farmed, we managed to get by with out using too many pesticides, sure I used them years ago a bit, but soon changed my ways and have been trying my darnedest to get things changed ever since. Reason being, I didn't have to look too far in seeing what it can do to folks. One being my old Dad, the person I loved so much, as pesticides is what brought his life to an end by contributing to his leukemia.

"'Thing is folks, we need these insects and things that are here on this old earth, good and bad." Everything that was put here was put here for a reason. I for the life of me can't see why some folks can't see what is going on, as through my eyes it's as clear as looking at a fifty foot wall, right in front of ones nose.

Well I guess I should say I know why these things are happening, as in my books and I say this again, it all boils down to money, money, money. If we keep this up though, money will be no good to anyone, as there won't be anyone around to spend it. Don't get me wrong, I am not writing this to hurt anyone. What I am writing this for, is that I am hoping that folks will start to see the light a wee bit and realize that money isn't everything and we should be looking after our health and well being.

I figure it this way. If I can get just one person to stop spraying their lawn, trees, driveway, gardens and things, I then would have saved a few million insects. In doing so, that few million insects can then get on with their work in pollinating crops and things, which leads to us humans having a healthy life.

Wouldn't it be nice for your young ones to be able to go out in your garden, dig in the dirt and have some fun, pesticides free? Or just being able to have a homegrown juicy tomato without washing it, chemical free. Or just to sit out in your back yard on the sweet smelling grass and being able to take a deep breath. Well, the only way this is going to happen, is that some of us humans are going to have to change our ways.

So there you have it, a bit on how I feel about what is going on in today's world. Tomorrows world, well that's up to you.

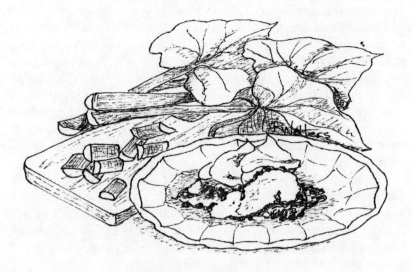

Rhubarb

Another vegetable that is real easy to grow and that every one should have in their gardens, is Rhubarb. I gotta' say, other than tomatoes there isn't anything that I enjoy more. Most folks today don't even eat it anymore. Us older folks though growing up, couldn't wait till spring arrived so we could get that first rhubarb pie.
Also very good for your Diboliconstatution, yep, I said that. Pretty well the only big word I ever use.

You know, you can grow rhubarb almost anywhere, myself I just incorporated it in amongst my vegetable gardens, along with a bit more around a tree out front of our home. It loves to grow up against something I have found, like a barn, post, tree, even a fence. Guess it don't like being alone, kind of like us humans. Another way of how it portrays us humans, is that it has a good side and a bad side. It can be very tasty, but remember this; Rhubarb Leaves, contain high amounts of oxalic acid. If ingested, your heart will stop and you will die. Amazing isn't it, how something that can be so good for you, yet also be so harmful.

Rhubarb doesn't take too much looking after either and once it gets to growing, it can be dug up, broken into different sections, meaning the roots and then transplanted anywhere you like. Once you have one plant growing you will never have to buy anymore.

I have found that spring is the best time for planting. If you got a bit of good compost, or any kind of manure, give them a few handfuls and work it in around the newly planted roots. It will reward you within a couple weeks. Pretty good huh? Just for a few handfuls of manure and a few minutes of your time, amazing.

The best time to eat it is early in the spring, as I have found that it has a lot less acid in it at that time of year. For those that the acid doesn't bother, just keep it watered well throughout the summer months and you will be picking it regularly.

Just remember three things, the roots and the leaves are poison, the stalk is what you eat. Keeping that in mind, you are all set to enjoy a good healthy treat, I would say we should all eat it a few times each spring to keep the old body ticking away nicely.

My lovely wife cooks it up with a bit of sugar, then puts it in the fridge overnight. The next evening while reading a book or just relaxing playing a game of crib, out it comes and what a treat it is.

I should also say that rhubarb is not just for eating, it also is a very pretty plant for your gardens and compliments it in special ways. One can also make a good natural pesticide out of the leaves.

The way I make it, is I break off the leaves mid summer, as that is when you will need a bit of help once in awhile in your garden with some insects. Take them into your house and put them into a pot on the stove with a pint or two of fresh cold water, don't use water out of your hot water tank. A pound or so of leaves goes a long way. Bring to a boil for a minute then simmer for about twenty minutes. Allow to cool, then strain into a bowl and let sit for another hour or so on the counter. Once that is done, you can use up all them old pieces of hand soap that you have laying around in the bathroom, that is if they aren't a deodorant soap, ivory or just plain hand soap is great. Once you get the pieces gathered up, cut them up into slices real thin and dissolve them into the brew you just mixed up with the leaves. You can put the soap pieces in while it is cooling if you like, as it will speed up the process of dissolving the soap.

Once that is done, buy yourself a hand pump sprayer, which one can buy at their local hardware store. That's it, now just load up the brew you made and get to spraying anything that has some bugs on it. Just remember, don't spray everything all the time as most pests are good. The rule of thumb is, if you have bad insects usually given time, good insects come along and keep them at bay, no pesticides needed. But every so often you need help and this is a sure fire way of getting that help without using the store boughten stuff, which is deadly not only to insects, but to us humans too. With this old recipe the bugs move on without killing them.

So there you go, a bit on our Rhubarb plant and why I feel everyone should have a few plants growing, if not for eating, just to look at.

Last note: Never eat any fruit, plant or vegetable if you don't know what they are.

Tree Transplanting

When spring arrives here in the north I can't get outside fast enough.
One of the first things I like to do if needed is look around our property and
see if any transplanting needs to be done.

Since moving here to the north there has been this one beauty of a
hemlock growing, that my wife really loves. The only problem was, it was
growing up in amongst our pines and with out the right amount of sunshine,
its days were numbered.

I had given some thought on moving it for three years in a row, but
always something came up that distracted me and it just didn't get done. The
time came though that we were doing some cleaning up and things around
our old homestead and once finished, my wife said.

"You know George, where we just cleaned up would be a perfect spot for
that hemlock that I love so much." Hmm, well I knew how much she loved
that tree and it was not long for this world where it was growing now, so..... I
figured I would give it a try and see what I could do.

As it went we lucked out, as it had thawed enough around the roots and
being wet enough we were able to dig it out without too much of a struggle.
The way we went about it was, I kind of just hooked my wife up to the top

part of the tree letting her bend it over, while I dug up the roots. Worked slick and and in no time we were ready to replant it.

I know from years of experience that trees can be very tricky to get going when moving them, especially when they are over ten feet tall. The way I went about this was, I dug down about a foot or so and wide enough to accommodate all the roots. Main thing at this point is not to cramp the roots, give them lots of room in the new hole. Just before placing the tree into its spot, I like to take a few good shovel-fulls of cow manure and spread it out at the bottom of the hole, old compost would be fine too. Now one has to make sure to pick the nicest side of the tree and put that side out where folks will be taking in its beauty the most. I like to take my time here, standing back in different locations covering all angles, as this is the only chance one gets to get it right. Once I had it sitting in the hole, I then threw in another couple shovel fulls of cow manure, along with a pail of water or two then finishing it up with soil. "No chicken manure here, as it could burn the roots."

Last but not least, being a wild tree right out of the bush, one should take note of its former surroundings. Easy enough to do, and in doing so I found that the ground was covered with leaves and pine needles. So I gathered up a few wheelbarrow loads and spread it around the base of the tree, knowing that it would make it feel more at home, along with holding in the moisture when them warm days of summer arrives.

Well, my wife had her tree transplanted, I gave it a good pep talk about growing and the rest was left up to Mother Nature.

Swiss Chard

Another real tasty vegetable for the garden, is Swiss Chard, and in my books there is nothing more healthier for you. With their dark green leaves you just know you are getting everything you need, mineral and vitamin wise in your special salads that you will be having throughout them summer months.

Swiss Chard is a real simple crop to grow and I don't think any garden should be without them. We even put a few in the flower gardens out front of our home, as we like the look of them when they get to growing. There is no need to buy plants, as planting the seeds straight into your fresh worked soil will grow just fine.

I like to plant a row of around ten feet long, which will feed a family of four, three or four times a week all summer long.

I usually mark off my row with a stake at each end and run a piece of twine in between each one. I then just take my hoe and dig out a small trench about an inch deep, full length of the row. Now I like to add a light layer of fertilizer at the bottom of the trench. Grass cuttings is best or old compost, but if you don't have any, a sprinkle of 10-10-10 fertilizer will do just fine. Now just work it in a wee bit with your hands.

Once you got your row cut out and soil fertilized, it's time to get down on your hands and knees and sprinkle a wee bit of seed throughout the whole row. That's the way I do it, but if you get real energetic you can place each seed around a half an inch apart. Not really necessary though as the seeds will grow just fine, even if you sow it a bit too thick. You can thin them out a bit later on if you so wish.

Swiss Chard and most any vegetables like full sunshine if at all possible, so when you plan your vegetable garden, keep an eye on the sun and when you have found a spot that has sunshine for 90% of the day, that's where you will make your garden.

Watering is one thing you don't need to do a whole lot, but if you happen on a real dry year, I would give them a drink once a week just to keep them looking good.

Once they get up there aways and you have had a few meals, your taste buds will be asking for something different and the swiss chard will be put on the back burner, so to speak. When this happens the plants will start to get a few flowers starting on the top from not picking it as much. This is the time to cut the flowers off and thin them out a bit. Reason being, so that when the urge hits you again for a taste, you will have plenty of fresh leaves ready to go.

The nice thing about swiss chard is that it will last you right up into late fall.

The way we like to prepare it for eating, is to pick it just a few minutes before you want to cook it. We then just rinse the leaves in cold water and take them dripping from the tap and put them in a pot, no more water needed.

Most folks I have found over cook it and in doing so one looses a lot of it's goodness. So keep an eye on it and as soon as it is tender, take it off the heat immediately.

Once it's cooked we like to add a few fresh cloves of crushed garlic and a touch of butter, not margarine either. The only thing left to do now, is to put it on a plate and dig in, you are in for a feast, and so..... healthy for ya.

One last thing, come fall we usually have lots left, and, well, we hate to see it go to waste. When that happens my wife does up a bunch of fresh tomatoes from our garden. She then goes out and picks the last of the swiss chard, boils it lightly and mixes it with the tomatoes, then puts it in jars.

Come winter you then invite some good friends over for a spaghetti dinner and just before serving, pour a jar of tomatoes and chard over the top. I guarantee, once they have tasted it, they will be back for more and it will be on top of their list for their garden come spring.

Swiss Chard loves to grow near; cabbage, broccoli, cauliflower, onions, lettuce and herbs. They don't like to be planted next to string beans I have found.

Also remember this, Swiss Chard and other leafy vegetables are a good sources of folic acid, vitamins A, C and E and other components which helps boost the skin's natural defense against damage caused by UV rays. So, just one more reason to get out there and plant your own garden.

SELF-HEAL   YARROW   COMFREY

Weeds

You know a thought that has occurred to me more than once throughout my life, is why so many folks hate weeds. If one looks back through history, we would come to realize that a lot of man's medicines were made from plants, with a mixture of fact, folklore and superstition, thrown in for good measure. I recollect my old friend Grey Wolf saying;

> **Yellow plants were good for jaundice.**
> **Red ones, of course, for the blood.**
> **If leaves looked similar to the liver,**
> **they were used to treat liver ailments.**
> **If a plant or a brew smelled bad or tasted**
> **worse, it must be good for you.**

My old friend didn't always go by trial and error though, as he said one could just watch the animals and see how they coped with things in every day life. For example, if one animal got a rash from one plant he would watch and see what plant they would rub against to fix the problem.

Things like that were the foundation of our country years ago and for some parts they are still being practiced today, not enough mind ya in my books, as we could sure learn a lot from nature. Especially if we would just accept things for what they are. I am a firm believer that for every disease, nature has a cure, but the problem in finding that cure was that we didn't listen to our Elders and lots was lost. Certain things in life can't be taught in schools I have found, as it has to be handed down from generation to generation, something like farming.

I also have wondered why folks haven't mixed certain weeds in with their gardens of today. My wife and I like to take a few roots from the wild grasses and dig them in here and there, along with a few bull thistles. Now in mentioning these bull thistles one should know they are also a good test for our soil, to see if it's up to par. Reason being, bull thistles won't grow in poor soil, so if you plant a few and they grow, you know you can grow pretty well any vegetable you want. If it dies, you can bet your soil is lacking something.

Years ago my old Dad used to dig up thistles and plant them in with the grapes, kind of used them as a barometer you might say. They not only help us in recognizing good soil, they also look nice and isn't that what we all strive to have in our gardens, well I do anyways.

You know, old Mother Nature is here for all of us to enjoy, but some how a bit of the thinking in this world has got messed up in my eyes. Most folks of today just want to get rid of them anyway they can. I don't like to call them weeds at all, they are plants, like the ones you buy in the stores, not to mention that they are free.

Over the years I have had four main interests in my life, writing, farming, landscaping and woodworking. With all four of these I have tried to work what was given to us through nature, into each of them.

My wife, other than being an artist and many other traits throughout her life, was also a landscape designer and over the years she has designed hundreds of cottages and homes throughout Ontario. Every home she designed was done with Mother Nature looking over her shoulder, along with keeping things simple and beautiful.

On a final note. I have found that most folks will ignore natural medicines up until the day they run out of options. Reason I know, is that is what happened to my old Dad. They told him that there was no more anyone could do for his Leukemia and that's when he sought out a treatment in Mexico. Thing was he waited too long. I am not saying that the treatment in Mexico would have been the cure, but I feel that we should take a close look at some things before it becomes too late.

Most people only turn to herbs and natural medicine when their regular doctors say there is no more they can do for them. What a darn shame too, as I feel they have missed out on an opportunity that might have been as close as ones own back yard, Mother Nature.

Well there you go, and think about this. If every weed on earth was destroyed, what would happen to us humans? We would cease to exist.

Rabbit Problems

Critters don't usually bother my garden too often, but every once in awhile one or two comes along to test my tolerance. For example, one year I decided on planting a few raspberry bushes, which did quite well until a few pesky rabbits decided to put them on their menu. I didn't even think they liked them. I know some folks would say I could put them on my menu and solve my problem right quick. But other than them eating my plants, I kinda' like having them around, as I enjoy watching them. So with not wanting to hurt them, I decided to do some thinking and see if I could come up with a remedy.

What happened was, one day I was taking out the ashes from my wood stove and noticed that on one end the raspberries, they had just about cleaned them right off to the ground. They had done this before but not to this extent, so that got me looking a bit closer and what I found was not only rabbit tracks but deer tracks too. I think the reason for this was, that we had a cold wet spring, then came the warm dry summer, which caused things not to grow too well, which cut their food supply down a bit.

At any rate, I don't like to feed them too much, the deer that is, as we live sort of close to the highway and I would hate to see someone getting hurt by hitting one, not to mention what would happened to the deer.

I remember one year coming back from Florida going through the Blue Ridge Mountains, one ran out in front of our old car, and I got to tell ya, it sure did a lot of damage. The trooper got to talking to me after things settled down and told us that we were very lucky, as they usually jump when the lights are right upon them and a lot of times they go right through the windshield. Well that didn't happen to us, thank goodness, but it sure made us count our blessings.

We did get a kick out of one part of this dilemma, as after we hit the deer we were standing along the highway, which back then didn't have very many cars on it. Finally a Trooper pulled up and got out.

"See you hit a deer huh? Are you going to keep it?"

"Nope, I replied."

"Well......would you mind if I took it?"

"Help yourself," I said.

With that he walked over to the deer, drug it up on to the road by his car and threw it on the hood. Then without even saying good-bye, he was gone. I looked at my wife and she looked at me, both thinking, well, now what do we do.

Ended up he was back in about fifteen minutes, but gotta' say it had us thinking there for a bit. But in thinking about this, back then in small towns they did things different than most. It also kind of gets a person to thinking of how things has changed in todays world. Some of the small towns still cater to some of the old ways like where we live now, but I got a feeling change is in the works. Hope I am wrong.

I always remember my old Grandfather saying,

"George, beware of new folks that move to town that want to change things," lot of truth in them few words.

We did get our car fixed up the next day after hitting that deer, with the help of some town folks and was soon heading on down the highway.

Back to them pesky rabbits and deer that were eating my raspberries. The more I got to thinking about it, a thought came to me, maybe the answer to the problem was there with me all the time. "Ashes." I decided to take hands full of the ashes and throw it on top of the leaves and stalks of the bushes. Well got to tell ya, never had another one eat one leaf or stalk again. I guess they didn't like the stuff on their feet, or the taste, but either way they are leaving them alone which is to my liking.

So now I am thinking, since it worked for the berry bushes so well, it would probably work for other things too. Amazing what can come to a person if one just takes the time to sit back and do some thinkin' huh?

So there you go, thought I would share, as nothing worse than doing all that work in growing things, just to loose it all to a few bunny rabbits and a couple deer.

Sweet Well Water

Another great thing about living in the north, is that most of us have good drinking water. I often wonder how many folks get up each morning and never give it a second thought. My wife and I was very fortunate when moving here to the north, as we lucked out with a real good drilled well.

Back on the farm we had pretty good water, just it had a heavy taste to it and never rightly figured out what caused it. Seemed that when you took a drink, it felt like it was thick or heavy or something. We tested it of course and the results came back good, but just the same, it took some getting use to. Not so now where we live, as our water is so good tasting that it makes you want to come back for a second glass and so.......cold, year round.

For years when my Dad was alive we used to go to market each week and along one old highway there used to be two nice spots where a fellow could pull the truck over and get a cool drink. Sure tasted good on a hot day and with just a cup or two, a fellows thirst, soon left him.

There was another spot that was on our route each week, but as the traffic got heavier the highway got larger and it was covered up with pavement.

Most of these were artesian wells, some small in size, but when drilled, pressure from within pushed the water up and out. One thing about them, a pump was never required that's for sure and if one was lucky enough to have one on their property, well lets say, they were set for life.

One artesian well I remember, was at my Dads cottage here in the north. When building the cottage he dug down a few feet with the back hoe and water came pouring out. Ended up he had to make a ditch so the water would have a place to run. Luckily the cottage was right near a lake, which saved us a lot of digging. Always liked going to that cottage, was away from everything and one could relax at any given time of day. Just thinking about it brings back some fond memories of my old Dad, sure miss him. Today though its been built up all around and the privacy is all but gone. The water is still running but contaminated and unfit for drinking, sign of the times, folks around there say.

Come to think of it, most of all the old wells I knew of, are either contaminated or covered up. Too bad too, as some folks will never get a taste of good drinking water, that comes right out of the ground. Myself I hate the taste of city water, never could get used to drinking it. For a few years we used to visit some friends of ours that lived in the city. It seemed that every time I had a shower at their home I ended up with a rash a few days later. My wife said the water made her skin bumpy. At any rate we never found out what caused the rash or my wifes skin being bumpy, we just chalked it up that our bodies got spoiled with our good old well water.

I often wonder if my old Dad was alive, what he would say with us selling water in stores, and people actually buying it. Something that should have and would have been safe and free, if we would have taken a bit more care. Some say it's called progress, had to happen, but not this old feller.

The thing about nice fresh well water, is that it comes with a lot of things in it that the old body needs. If one had a good well today or access to one, I bet we could cut down half of our visits to the doctor each year, if not more. Reason being, that the water is loaded with minerals and good things, that keep us healthy and strong. I know most folks say, well water is unsafe, I say get it tested and enjoy.

I had a friend once that had weak bones, or so they told him at the doctors office. Well he got to thinking and moved from the city to the country, all the time figuring on finding a place with good water on the property. Took a bit of work, but he ended up finding a place. Well he got to drinking six to ten glasses of cold well water each and every day. About two years later the doctor said he should have his bones tested again, as they were probably getting pretty bad since his last visit. He tried to tell them that he felt a lot better, but to keep them happy he went in for the test. Once the results came in, the doc called him into his office and said.

"I can't explain it, but your bone test came back looking great, looks like a twenty year old." The old feller didn't say anything, just smiled and left.

I got to thinking about that and if one really looks at it, it makes sense. Drinking good wholesome water with all the minerals in it, put back in what he had lost over the years, seems logical to me.

Yep a lot of folks are out of luck today, in getting good drinking water, but for myself and my family, each and every morning when we get up, we walk over to the tap and in about ten seconds out comes crystal clear ice cold water, something not to be taken for granted.

Benefits Of Drinking Fresh Well Water

1-Improves Your Energy
2-Increases Your Mental and Physical Performance
3-Removes Toxins & Waste Products from your body
4-Keeps Skin Healthy and Glowing
5-Helps You Lose Weight
6-Reduces Headaches and Dizziness
7-Allows for proper Digestion

My wife has always said, that the things that are the most important in life, is for free and you know, she is right.
So there you go, a wee bit on one item that the old guy upstairs, gave us lots of for free, and what did we do with it?

But on a happy note, if you happen by our home, drop in and I will pour ya all a cold drink of sweet well water, no charge.

Sayings

Years ago we had a few good sayings on the farm, and well I thought I would share some.

Late in the day when Reg was bringing in the cows I can almost here him saying. "I gotta' say George, it's so cold the gates wouldn't hardly open to let the cows in from the fields."

Another good old saying which brought back memories was from Laura while cooking in the kitchen.

"One has to be always on guard she would say, when it comes to making bread and things, if it's too cold the yeast won't rise, if it's too hot it will die."

A fellow up the road aways, that I went to visit once in awhile, by the name of Jim, well I got to say that if you didn't know him, you would think he was the most cantankerous person on earth. But once you did get to knowing him like I did over the years, one would find he was a big old softy inside. One day Laura asked me to take a couple loaves of fresh home made bread over to his place, as he did a lot of things for us, especially in haying season.

I enjoyed the ride on Jennie my horse and having to go through the back country of our property which was mostly bush made it that much better, as I don't think there was ever a prettier place. To make it even better, over the years Reg had made logging roads all through the bush, which sure made riding a lot easier.

Well I got to Jim's place and he was out by the barn breaking a hole through the ice in the watering trough so that his horses could get a drink.

"Hey Jim I hollered, how's it going? I brought you over some home made bread fresh out of the oven, Laura wanted you to have it."

He looked up and said. "Well don't set there jawing all day, get down from that there horse and lets go in by the fire and get to eating it."

Once in the house we took off our coats and hung them on a nail by the stove. He then got out some holders which were actually made from coat hangers. He cut off some slices of the bread and laid them on the top of these holders, opened one lid on the cook stove and held the bread over the flame. In a bit they turned a nice shade of brown, he buttered them up and poured a bit of his Home Grown Honey over them, we then got to eating. I gotta' tell ya, it sure was good. I think I could have eaten a whole loaf, but two pieces was all I got.

While eating I remarked on how cold it was outside, well Jim looked up and scratched his head and said.

"Yep sure is cold out there, it's so cold that folks are going to church just to hear about the fires of hell." I looked over at him and we both got to laughing.

"Now don't you go running back and mention to Laura on what I said there young feller, she being so God fearing and all?" I told him not to worry, I wouldn't say a thing.

I did let it slip though a year or so later one day, while out feeding the cows around the middle of winter. I remember Laura looking over at me and said.

"I bet you got that saying from old Jim up the road didn't ya? Crazy old fool, one of these days,"....... and she stopped herself from saying the rest.

Another saying thinking back was one summers day, we were out in the barn Reg and myself gathering eggs. Reg had taken out his handkerchief to wipe off his brow as the sweat was running in his eyes.

"Sure is a hot one, huh Reg?"

"Hot" he said, "it's so hot out there that these eggs we are gathering are probably all hard boiled."

Yep back when, things were simpler to my way of thinking, things that folks said and done had meanings, not words like today that's for sure. When a woman or a man spoke to a young one, he or she knew right off what they meant, no fuss or questions asked.

I sure miss them days, and in my eyes we sure wouldn't be hurt any, if we brought back into being, at the very least, a few of them.

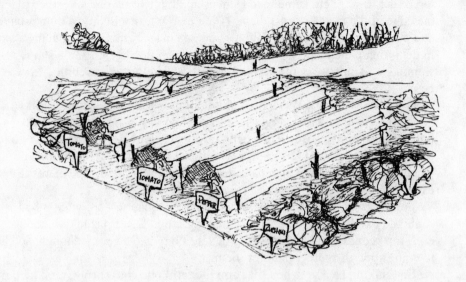

Frost Protection

Come spring the first thing I think about is gardening, but close behind that is frost. Over the years I have tried different ways in dealing with it, so figured I would share some of those ideas.

First thing one should do is keep a close eye on the weather. Only problem one would have there, is that the locations of the Governments weather stations are usually miles away from where one lives. Results being that not living close to their stations the weather can be quite different. Like where my wife and I live, as usually we are a few degrees warmer which is a good thing, most of the time but occasionally it's the opposite.

One easy way of finding out about frost in your area, is to check the Dew point temperature between noon and one each day and usually that temperature reading will give you approximately the low for that night. Knowing that and if the temperature says it is close to the freezing mark, it would be advisable to get yourself out there and cover up your newly planted gardens before retiring for the evening.

I remember one year after we moved here to the north, I had my garden all planted early, I guess my inner feeling that usually tells me the right time to plant, kind of slipped up. So....... I had to come up with a quick plan to fix things.

The long rows of tomatoes was quite simple, as I had some eight foot long sheets of aluminum that I took off my old shop. Glad I saved them now and what I did was, as they bend real easy, I made sort of a dome over the top of the rows. I cut some wood stakes and put two on one side, then placed the edge of the metal against them. Then bent it as I said, into a dome shape and put in two more pegs to hold it, worked slick. Now I can leave the stakes in the ground and just remove the metal through the day when the sun is shinning and quickly put them back before retiring for the evening, if need be.

If you don't have any sheets of aluminum, which I suspect most folks don't, one could buy them eight foot long vinyl or plastic sheets I would think at any lumber yard. They bend easily also and one wouldn't have to lay out a whole lot of money and they would last for years. No more rolls of plastic or tarps to buy, which has a tendency of breaking off the plants if not careful.

For my rows of radishes and other things that had just sprouted, I had some old eave troughs that had been laying around, so I just laid them up each row, couldn't ask for anything better. Only had a couple though, so had to come up with another plan for the rest.

So thinking back to when I was on the farm one cold spring, reminded me of how I hilled up each side of the rows with soil, then covered the small spouts with straw, saved our crop for the year. So I figured it worked then, why not now, and hilled up all the rows. I then went into the bush and gathered up a bunch of leaves spreading them lightly over the top of the sprouts, which worked out great.

That looked after my one garden up by the house, but down below our home I made another garden where I planted around sixty tomato plants. What I did there was I cut a couple pieces of two by fours, about four feet long. Put a point on one end and a V cut on the other end. I then took them down to the garden, drove them into the ground, one at each end. I then laid a long thin pipe I had laying around into the V, kind of like a ridge pole one would use on a truck, to hold the tarp.

I then stretched out the tarp over the whole thing and pegged each side into the ground, which gave me a roof effect look. Worked great and no way the frost could get down to my plants.

The last thing to cover was my cucumbers. Having them planted in hills ended up being a good thing, as I just took some big old leaves of rhubarb and laid them on the top of the young sprouts, worked slick.

I know one would think that is a lot of work, but if one gets things together and puts them away, the next time is a snap and don't forget, they will not only come in handy for spring but you will be able to harvest your crops longer when them cool fall days arrive.

So there you have it, a bit on how to look after them tender vegetables, when nature just doesn't want to play along with ya.

How My Elders Told The Weather

One of my most favorite hobbies throughout my life, has been keeping an eye on the weather.

Over the years I have always kept an eye on the sky and the ground for that matter, in deciding what the weather was going to be for the day.

There are a number of ways to tell the weather and for most folks they just turn on the television or radio. For me though I was taught different ways. For example, if you look at the clouds and see they look a lot like a mares tail on a horse, you know it is the leading front of a storm or rain.

If there is a haze around the moon at night, it usually means rain or in coming bad weather for the next day.

Old Grey Wolf taught me a few different ways, like while walking along and you spot ant hills, with sand like dirt piled high around their holes.

"Sure sign of rain," he would say. He also taught me that when the leaves on the trees showed their bellies, rain was not too far off.

The squirrels loading up with nuts and pine cones, meant a cold or long winter. Crows returning to an area, were a sign of spring and if the first Robbin you seen, was flying, or up in a tree, well, that meant a prosperous year. Thinking about that, the ones I have spotted over the years have been on the ground, but my wife has always come to my rescue as hers have been up off the ground. So between the both of us, we get a medium-yolker of a year.

For years now I have kept sort of a journal on the weather and for most parts it is just for my amusement. But I have also used it when figuring out when to plant crops and things. For example, I would never plant my vegetables until after the full moon in May. Reason being, is that if you are going to get a frost, that will be when it most likely happens, with it being a clear sky and all.

Now I am not into too many technical things and pretty well rely on the old ways. But with two sons that are into these high tech items of today, one has to lean a wee bit, to their way of thinking.

So one year, Karl my youngest son, being an Electronics Technologist, set my computer up with a weather station. It is situated up on a pole just behind our house, logs data and sends it to my computer. Pretty nice to have and to take it one step further, he made me a web site. He then set my computer up so it collects the data and sends it to our web site for folks to see. The thing I like the most about it is, that it gives me a daily 12 hour forecast and stores the data and whenever I want to look back at a year, it is only a click away.

Now in saying all this, I still don't just rely on the weather station. I usually take notes on what nature is doing and then put everything together and come up with my own report. I then like to compare it with the weather station, and over the years, I have found my personal forecasts have been pretty well right on.

Yep times have changed over the years, some for the good I would say, but it sure is a shame that a lot of the old ways of doing things are all being forgotten. The part that hurts me the most though, is that most of the ways of the past has not been kept up. Our elders have been put out to pasture so to speak, and folks of today don't think their wisdom is needed anymore.

I often wonder what would happen if we had a major disaster. Years ago our elders knew how to handle problems as they arose. The reason they could handle these problems, was that they learned from what their elders had taught them and was able to put their learnings into practice if needed.

One has to remember, that not everything can be taught in schools. I have found, that the most important things in life has to be handed down from generation to generation, like farming for one. I know I keep on saying that, but it's so true. Miss one generation and we are in serious trouble.

Today I kind of think folks have gotten to rely on others, instead of themselves, and this is not a good thing.

My advice if asked could be summed up with four words. Listen to your elders.

For my wife, myself, and two boys, we have listened to our elders, we learned what we needed to know, and as my father before me, we shall survive.

Potato Storage

Years ago just down the road aways from our dairy farm, lived some real nice folks. They made their living growing potatoes. Reg occasionally went for a visit and if I had my chores done, I would tag along. Thinking back we never went without potatoes, reason being we would trade off different things for a few bags throughout the year.

I gotta' say, they sure tasted good back then. I suppose it was because of them being just picked, not being in cold storage, or not being sprayed with all kinds of chemicals, like todays potatoes. The ones in the stores today are kept in paper bags, which isn't a real good thing, at least to my way of thinking. They do have a venting system worked into the bags, but sure doesn't work too well. The paper that they use, soaks up all the moisture which holds it, and the potatoes never really dry out. Damp or wet potatoes goes bad pretty fast if left for any length of time.

Today what I would suggest for folks that don't grow their own, would be to look up a farmer that sells them and go and see them. That way one knows they are always getting fresh produce.

If you happen upon a farmer that still does things the old way, you will probably get your potatoes in a burlap bag, which is the best. I think all potatoes for long time storage should be stored in burlap bags. If you can't find any it would be best to just take them out of the paper bags they come in and leave them loose in a wooden bin.

My wife and I grow our own, but every once in awhile throughout the early part of the season we run out. If this happens we then have to buy a bag or two. If they happen to be in paper bags, as soon as we get them home we take them out and put them in burlap, as I always have a few laying around. You will be surprised how long they will keep.

Some say that storing onions and potatoes together is a bad thing, that they give off some gas or something that causes them both to spoil quicker. My view on this subject is that the two seem to like different temperatures.

So with that in mind I kept an eye on things and found that my cold room is good for potatoes and other veggies, but my onions didn't do so well. Finding that out, I now just hang my bags of onions in another room, where it's cool and dry.

Our cold room is quite simple, as we took a corner in one end of our basement, away from the furnace room and built a small room. I would say about five feet by five feet would be its size and about six feet tall. We then cut a hole through the basement wall and run a ten inch piece of plastic pipe through to the outside. On the outside of the pipe we fastened on a screen, so no critters could get in. On the inside we took a lid off an old can, put a screw through its top and into the plastic pipe, which now acts like a small gate. We now can open the hole in the pipe all the way, half way or what ever we want, to get the correct temperature.

To make sure we had the right temperature, we just hung a thermometer inside the cold room, that way we can keep an eye on things. Works slick, and I think every home should have one, easy to do and you will save hundreds of dollars a year. We store everything in ours, and not only vegetables. Coffee, lard, butter, oils, canned goods, even soft drinks for when the kids come visiting.

You also will have to insulate the walls and ceiling a wee bit, but that is real easy to do. Just pick up some one inch Styrofoam. The pink kind actually works the best, as it is a bit more resistant to moisture.

Last thing you should put in is a light, as it can be quite dark in there and usually supper is when you will be needing something.

I know some say, boy that is a lot of work just to store a few items. But really it isn't, as a long weekend would be all that is required to build one. Not to mention what the benefits would be in savings each year. Also you are becoming a wee bit more self efficient, and in my books, that isn't a bad thing to be doing in today's world.

In growing potatoes they also like the company of other vegetables and flowers, here are a few; Beans, Cabbage, Corn, Eggplant, Horseradish, Lettuce, Marigolds, Onions, Peas and Petunias.

You shouldn't plant them near; Melons, Rutabagas, Squash, Sunflowers, Tomatoes or Turnips.

Also remember this. Minerals in potatoes are very important in the bodies defense against diseases. The vitamin C in freshly dug potatoes is quite high, but once stored for around 9 months it drops to about half, still good though.

Cooking potatoes that isn't peeled conserves most of the vitamin B, C and salts. Peeling a potato before it is boiled reduces its vitamin content considerably. So......what does that tell ya? Well it tells me to get out there come spring and get to planting, as that is a sure fire way of getting all the goodness out of my vegetables that I can possibly get.

We eat a lot of potatoes in our diet, not that we over do it, but my lovely wife has all kinds of recipes using potatoes. She makes the best potato soup I have ever tasted.

One last reminder, if you do build a storage for your potatoes and start storing them, make sure you get them out of the paper bags as soon as possible, and never buy washed potatoes.

If you grow your own, leave some dirt on them when digging, as a little dirt will about double their time in storage.

Wife's Potato Soup Recipe

Boil five or six potatoes with a piece of salt pork and a little celery.

Pass through a colander and add milk or cream, (if you use milk add a bit of butter) to make the consistency of thick cream.

Cut a little parsley fine and throw in.

Let boil five minutes.

Cut some dry bread diced and fry till brown in color in hot lard or olive oil.

Drain them and place them in the bottom of a soup tureen. (Sorry forgot, old school.) Bottom of a soup bowl.

Then pour the soup over the top. If you like onions, add them to the soup and boil for a bit longer, then pour it over the top.

That's it and I gotta' tell ya, just thinking about it got my mouth to watering.

One Special Pumpkin

You know every once in awhile certain things have a way of gettin' to a fellow, for example.

One spring I got to putting in my two vegetable gardens. In saying that, finding the right spot for a garden is something not to be taken lightly, as one has to make sure they are out in full sun all day long.

I kind of think now all my spaces are used up as most of my property is surrounded by huge pines and I sure wouldn't want to take them down, being so beautiful and all. Every once in awhile I like to sit and put my back up to one and try and visualize what they would have seen through their life time of growing. Crazy in some folks minds I suppose, but hey, I am a writer and I am different than most.

Once I found my spot for a garden I decided on putting in some corn, as the piece I choose was long and narrow. At the base of the corn I decided on putting in some companion plants, which ended up being three different kinds of squash. I gotta' tell ya, did they grow. I had corn like you wouldn't believe, and squash, well lets just say, I had a wheel barrow full for my cold room come fall.

On each end of the row I decided to see if I could grow some watermelon which did quite well considering that I got the seeds in a bit late. Only thing was, I had a pesky old raccoon that felt he deserved them before me, before they were even ripe actually. So guess I won't be planting any more of them, unless I put them up close to the house where I can keep an eye on them.

But one of the main things about this story is about a pumpkin that grew all on it's own. Well I did discard a couple old pumpkins the year before and I guess one seed manage to make it through winter and decided to grow on its own. Thing was the spot it picked was right in the middle of my pathway which ran from my house to the garden.

My first mowing of the season I cut it off by accident and in doing so I figured it was done for. I got busy after that with other things and didn't get back down to the lower garden for a week or so. When I did I couldn't believe it, that pumpkin plant that I cut off was growing to beat the band.

I can't have it right in the middle of my pathway I though, but then being a bit sentimental, I decided to just drag the vine off to one side. Bad mistake as I only ended up breaking it off. Well, I didn't really want that to happen, I said to myself, but it did, so, the bright side was, that now it is out of my way.

A couple weeks later I was down watering and low and behold that pumpkin was growing again, out in bloom this time, I couldn't believe it. This time I took extra caution in moving it but some how my leg got caught up in the vine and broke it off again. Darn I said to myself that pumpkin sure wanted to grow. Well, old saying goes, three times and out and I figured it was done for this time.

Spring carried on into summer and a few weeks later I was back watering and what did I see, yep that pumpkin was back up with two huge flowers. I then decided that this pumpkin wanted to grow and who was I to deny its rights. So I did without my pathway for the rest of the summer and left it alone.

Throughout the summer the flower turned into a pumpkin and grew it did. It wasn't the biggest one I ever grew, but the color, well it couldn't get any deeper orange. As fall arrived I got to thinking about using it for our porch for Halloween, which we did.

Cold weather arrived a bit later and I just didn't have the heart to throw it out, after all that it went through. I kind of figured that it had a purpose in life, so down in the cold room it went. Then one day in November the wife got me to bring it up and set it on the counter.

"Pumpkin pie," she said, "this pumpkin has found it's destiny."

"That suits me," I replied, "pumpkin pie with fresh whipped cream."

Even then I couldn't just let it go and before the wife got to making pies, I snapped a picture or two. The final goodbye was taking a few of its seeds and putting them away. Never know one might just happen to fall out of my pocket come next spring. Amazing what some plants can take in their struggle to live, something like us humans. Wouldn't you think?

Pumpkins like to grow near; Corn, Eggplants, Marigolds, Onions and Radishes. They don't like growing next to Potatoes.

One also should remember that pumpkin seeds have a great medicinal record in helping with; Bladder Function, Prevention of Osteoporosis, Natural Anti-Inflammatory, Prevention of Kidney Stones, Lowers Cholesterol, Cancer Prevention, and also helps in the Prevention of Heart Disease.

So as you can see, by just planting a few seeds, good health is just around the corner. Just another reason to get you out into the garden.

REAL PUMPKIN PIE

1 cups of fresh pumpkin pulp
2 eggs
2/3 cup sugar
1 1/2 cup milk
1/4 teaspoon of ginger
1/4 teaspoon of cloves
1 teaspoon of cinnamon
touch of salt

Mix until smooth, then pour into an unbaked 8-inch pie shell. Bake at 350 degrees for one hour, or until set. The pie will be paler than a pie made with canned pumpkin and will have a custard-like layer at the bottom. That's it. Enjoy!

Fall Is In The Air

Fall is a another one of my favorite times of year. When November
arrives I then start to relax a bit knowing I made it pretty well through
another year. Oh there is work that still has to be done, but I always figure
what work does come after November, if need be can wait.

One job that I enjoy doing is getting my firewood piled for winter. I like
getting it in the winter and piling it outside for most of the summer. I then
get busy and start bringing it into the basement, usually around fourteen
cords of good hardwood, as that seems to be the magic number for this old
house where we live now

My wood goes in around the end of August, as any later than that the
rainy damp weather sets in, at least for our area. I have also found that dry
firewood acts sort of like a wick, and sucks up dampness fast if left
uncovered for any length of time. If that happens, one then has to get it dry
again which can take some doing if it happens to be late in the season.

A bit of dampness doesn't bother me too much though, because as soon
as I light up the old wood furnace any dampness that is in the firewood is
gone in a day or so. A good sign that firewood is ready for burning is that
once you can see the cracks in the ends taking shape, you know you are in for
some good winter heat.

Some folks don't like the wood being brought into the house, but for
myself I just love it. No trudging through the snow, no wet wood, no

freezing in the early morning hours or throughout the night when one forgot to bring in enough. Only way to go.

The important part of having wood inside your home is to get it in at the right time of year, as I said above and only bring in good, clean, hardwood, not old rotten stuff.

On another note, fall is the time of year to get the gardens cleaned up. One has to remember that this time of year is every bit as important as in the spring. Once I get the garden itself cleaned up, I put the bagger on the mower and gather up all the leaves I can find. If I am lucky I usually manage to cover my garden about a foot thick.

Once that is all done up I usually have a bucket or two of good hardwood ashes from the furnace and throw it over top of the leaves. Make sure there isn't hot coals in there though or one might end up loosing all his or her hard work.

I also like to take my old corn stocks or any other thing that grew in my garden that is a bit too large to work in, and lay them all in a row on the ground. I then raise my mower up to its highest level and a little at a time, run over it. This chops it up nicely, and I have a bunch more good stuff to add to the garden.

Once this is all done and I am sure I have gathered up all I can find around the place, I then take out my rototiller and go over it once or twice. What this does, it mixes things up a bit, stops things from blowing away and also lets it rot easier throughout the winter months. Amazing how that works, as come spring all them leaves and things after tilling it up one more time, are all gone and becomes part of the soil that is in your garden. One can't ask for anything better than that. If one did that every fall there would be hardly no need for any fertilizer at all throughout the growing season.

After that is done if you are thinking like I am, it's time to pick up some garlic from a market, preferably some that is home grown. The kind I like, is when looking at it, it has a bluish tinge to it. Now when the weather says it's going to get cold out, say around the end of October, it's time to get it underground.

Real old saying and so true is, if you want to stay healthy, then don't forget the garlic. Also if you dream that garlic is in your home. It means good luck is heading your way.

So there you go, a bit on getting things ready for winter and once that is done, well, I sort of like to hibernate inside, where its nice and warm. Then when a craving hits, as they do, I then get to enjoying all them nice preserves, that my lovely wife has done up throughout the growing season. Tough life, huh?

Here are some hardwoods I like to use for firewood.

Ash, Beech, Yellow Birch, White Birch, Hickory, Sugar Maple..

The Old Subsoiler

Years ago most things were done a lot different than today. One item that comes to mind is the old subsoiler. All it was actually, was a long steel tooth which is curved in at the bottom. It would be hooked up to the three point hitch on the back of the tractor and as you moved forward it sunk into the ground. Just watching it, one wouldn't think it did much, but in reality it did a lot of good.

What it did was, it loosen the ground to a depth of around two feet. I used to run it along the top end of our grape rows each fall, as our farm was located midway up the escarpment. Kind of on a slope you might say. What happened was, the water would run off the escarpment and down the grape rows in the spring, leaving the earth a soupy mess. Problems then arose as I couldn't get onto the land with the tractors, and, well, if that happened I couldn't get my spraying done or the soil worked up. So I came up with the idea of running the subsoiler across the top of the whole Grapery, which loosened the ground and let the water run off go down in the trench I made, and no more problem. Worked slick.

I used that old subsoiler for a number of things. I remember my Dad and I one spring had to plant around five acres of new grape-vines. It is quite a job planting large acreage, as one has a lot of digging and bending over to do. So one night after giving it some thought my old Dad came up with a plan to weld up some steel plates onto the subsoiler. Ended up looking like, a V in

117

shape. We then welded a seat on just behind the V, and a place to put ones feet in front of the V. Then we welded up a bin on one side of the V to hold the grape-vines. "Hope you are able to get my meaning." It then was hooked to the tractor, and with Dad driving and me sitting on our new invention, out to the field we went.

I put enough young grape-vines in the basket which we made and Dad headed the tractor up the new row which we had marked out. He sunk the subsoiler down in the ground the depth that we needed for planting and as he drove along I dropped the vines in between the V we welded up, which sat between my legs. Worked great I will say that, and we planted the whole five acres in one day, with time to spare.

Over the years it caught on and eventually even the equipment dealers were making them for folks to buy. I always said too bad we didn't take out a patent on the thing. Oh well live and learn and if nothing else, we made a lot of farmers plantings a lot easier.

Moving here to the north and after getting settled, I put in a good size garden and after a year or so I found that my gardens was dry at the top end come summer and damp near the bottom. So thinking back about the old subsoiler I decided on making a trench a few feet just above my garden plot. Ended up I now got a garden which is pretty well all equal in wetness throughout the whole season. Reason being the trench at the dry end stops the water from running away and holds it back for a spell.

Yep, a lot of old farmers of years ago were pretty smart fellows, had to be, as it was the only way to survive.

Most of all our farm equipment of years past and today were invented by an old farmer. Sure some have been improved on, but the initial piece came from the mind of some wise old feller.

Today though we rely on computers you name it for our ideas. Some call it progress, me, well I won't elaborate on what I think.

So there you go a bit on one piece of equipment that came our way, through the mind of a farmer that decided, that with a bit of thought and imagination, things could be made to make his days work a lot easier, and mine too.

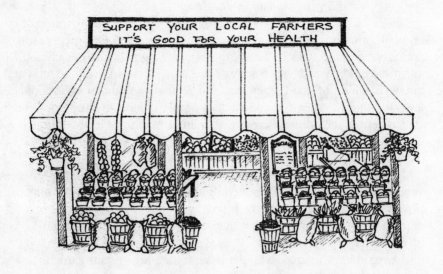

Farm Life

Farming today is a lot different than when I was farming. Some of the new ways are for the good but some I figure isn't so good. For example.

Years ago my old Dad and I grew all kinds of different fruit and vegetables. Reason being that if one crop didn't do so good, we had another to rely on. Today most farmers put all their eggs in one basket and then when a problem arises like bad weather or too many imports, then they are in trouble.

Also years ago we had huge privately owned wineries. They didn't have their own so to get their grapes to make wine they bought up pretty well all the grapes us farmers could grow.

I remember loading the truck, driving to the winery and sitting in line all night, so I would be one of the first to be unloaded and could get back home to work on the farm.

The canning factories also helped out back then and took quite a few grapes and other fruits, but they slowly got phased out, because with all the imports they couldn't compete anymore. Too bad too, as we sure had some good produce. There was a few that hung on, but eventually they had to close their doors also. Put a lot of hard working folks out of work too.

On our farms we had quite a mixture of fruit which was a good thing, but it was still a constant battle in seeking out new places to sell it. My Dad and me both had our own farmers market we went to and I got to say we made most of our money there. When times were tough though, we sold along side the road or highways and even delivered from house to house. I guess you could say we did what we had to do.

Times have changed though and for most parts it is pretty rough out there in the farming business today. Even though I am out of it now, I can honestly say I still miss it. Farming is something that is in ones blood, you either have it or you don't. Sure, we had a lot of hard-times, the wife and I, but we had a lot of good times too. I have always said that one should enjoy the work that is put before you each day and not have to struggle through it.

Up here in the north where my wife and I live now we are enjoying life to the fullest. We have slowly fixed up the old place we bought and every day we are adding new plants and things to our gardens.

If one really wanted to, they could pretty well grow most of all their own vegetables. It doesn't take a bunch of land to do it either. Most folks have flower gardens and if they did a bit of switching around, as I said in a couple other stories here and there, that they could fill them with all different kinds of fruits and vegetables.

I have always figured, why not have something in your gardens that you can eat, enjoy and look at too. That makes more sense to me, not to mention the savings one would have.

I was chatting with a young couple one time and they mentioned dieting and exercising and how much they hated it. Later on in our chat they asked how my wife and I kept so slim. I told them we don't diet or exercise at all, we eat natural and mostly unprocessed foods. The only exercise we get is shop work, gardening and the things that pop up around and in the house each day. All put together I told them, when night comes along we are ready for bed.

They then asked my feelings of how the young farmers compare to the old farmers. Well I scratched my head a bit and came up with this.

"There's a fine shine to the world when ones young. Your dreams are big and they reach to hell an' gone, and there ain't anything life can throw at ya that you're afraid of. You can take on life without a thin dime in your pocket, and laugh at it. Takes age to soften up a man and make him cautious and afraid, and I guess I got to say I have softened up a bit and become more cautious over the years, sign of the times."

So, there you go, a bit on the way farming was and is going today and a wee bit on a couple other things.

Over the years I have found that the important things in life are, good health and waking up each morning with a clear mind. I would also like to mention this for those that have lost a loved one.

"They are only as far away as you allow them to be. So find a quite spot, and get to chattin'. Do what you feel comfortable with and that gives peace of mind."

Fences

Years ago in some parts of the country, fences were put up with the thinking of keeping the animals in, and in some cases it was to keep us humans out. If one would have happened by our farm years ago, they would have seen that our fences lined the different fields and pastures. Not that we really needed all the fences, but when we cleared off the land we needed a place to put all the rocks and we had tons of them.

When we purchased the land the first thing we had to do was clear off the trees, which went for firewood and some lumber. Not all of them mind ya, but a lot of them, as we needed room to build and to plant our crops. After the trees were taken down the stumps then had to be removed, and I gotta' tell ya it wasn't an easy chore. Once they were out of the way then came the removal of the rocks and things. The stone removal was a job also, as some of them were a pretty good size. The way we moved them was with a stone-bolt, (Farm Sled). Basically a flat wooden platform, made out of good hardwood, with flat runners on each side for it to slide on. We would then hook it up to the team of Clyde's and throw all the stones onto it. The real large rocks, boulders one might say, we used long steel bars to roll them onto the stone-bolt. We would then drag the load of stones to the fence line we had planned out and unloaded them. Starting with the bigger rocks on the bottom of course, ending up with the smaller ones on the top. Worked slick and them fences were there for a life time and after that.

Every time I get to thinking of them days it never ceased to amaze me how strong them old Clyde's were. No matter how many rocks we put on

121

that old stone-bolt them Clyde's never gave their job a second thought, amazing critters.

The rocks weren't the only items that were incorporated in with the fences, there was also the stumps that we had pulled out, or dug up and I gotta' say they gave it a unique look.

Throughout our years of farming, we had over fifty fence lines made out of stone and every year we added more to them, as every time we worked the land, more would show themselves. I still can see Reg bending over to pick up a rock or two every time he went for a walk through the fields, just became a habit over the years.

It has been years now since I lived on the dairy farm, but every once in awhile we drop by for a visit, as the road we take to see our boys goes right past the place. I usually stop up above the old homestead and look down upon the house and barn, and as my eyes scan the fields, the old stone fences seem to reach out to me saying, "I'm still here, glad you dropped by."

I have to say those fields produced a number of great crops in my day and them fence lines, boy, they still look good, even after all these years.

The only thing that made me kind of sad when giving the old place a look over, was the old beech wood bush that sat on one corner of the property. Years ago that bush was not to be touched, as Laura said it was hers and them trees would never be cut. She used to sit there in the summer months for hours on end, just taking in what Mother Nature had to offer.

Not too many of the trees remain today, as they have been cut down for other things. Too bad too, as it sure made the farm, but then again, different folks have different ideas and it is their farm now, not ours.

A lot of things back in my early days were left alone for just its beauty and no money would cause one to destroy it. Yep life and folks change I suppose, for the best? Well, I guess that is something that only you can answer.

Old Time Items

Y ou know I got to thinking the other day on some old time items that
use to be quite plentiful, and how we made use of them. Today a lot of
things are just thrown out, back in my day, nothing was thrown away, well
maybe a few things.

One item I remember was twine that we used on the farm for tying up the
grape-vines in the early spring. It was quite a job and usually women did the
most of it, as they had a knack that a man couldn't duplicate, no matter how
hard they tried.

A lot of patience was needed, as one had to bring up the arms of the
grape-vines, wrap them around the wires being careful not to break off the
buds and then tie them solid. For years we used twine that we bought in
huge rolls, which I would take and cut pieces of around six to eight inches in
length. Thinking about that, I sure cut a lot of twine in my day.

Other ways we got twine was from the dairy farmers, as most of them
back then had bales of hay or straw and the binder twine was used to hold the
bales together. The nice thing about it was that most farmers back then just
discarded most of it, or hung it in some back room. So when my old Dad and
I approached them about it, they were happy to let us have it.

We actually didn't take it for nothing though, as being the way my old
Dad was, he worked out a deal trading some fruit for it. Seemed to just
mushroom after that and ended up that we had enough to tie a 100 acre farm

each spring, which worked good for a time, but like everything else, binder twine was phased out, and we had to go back to buying it from the stores.

Eventually they even stopped making the twine and thin wire was brought into the picture. Dad didn't like it as well, as it had a tendency of cutting into the vine and killing it. One had to be very careful not to tie them too tight. Thing was with twine, it gave a bit, where wire didn't move an inch. There was hundreds of other things that was done with old binder twine that I could mention and maybe some day I will, in another story.

Another item that is pretty well gone now, is wooden baskets. For years on our farm we use to buy up thousands of them. Nothing was wrong with them, other than maybe having the wrong name. We fixed that problem real quick with a coat of paint and once done we just stamped our own name on them. Worked good for a lot of years till the powers that be stopped us, saying it was unsanitary. Can you believe that? What's unsanitary about them? They were made out of wood and lasted for years.

Now a days they have gotten folks all switched around to paper baskets, which last about one season if that and then are thrown away, such a waste.

Yep folks minds have been swayed in today's world and in my books it all has not been for the best either. So much is going to waste it saddens me every time I get to thinking about it.

My wife and I still use a lot of the older items in our every day life and it always gives me pleasure to hear about how some folks are still using them.

Some say, "George look at all them trees that have to be cut down to make them wooden baskets."

I say, "Look at them paper ones that they are making now, where do you think they come from, not to mention that most only last for one year if that."

Sign of the times they say, the old ways are no good anymore, one has to move on, or be left behind. Hmm.

Another item was old cement blocks, I remember years ago my Dad helped me build my first home. We got the basement dug out and ready for the walls when my Dad heard about this feller that had a whole mess of used blocks. Well we went to see about them and sure enough he had hundreds of them. Thing was they were all different sizes.

Well that didn't stop Dad, we backed up the old truck and loaded them all on. Once back at the building site we unloaded and a good friend of ours got busy and started to lay them. The inside was all placed, smooth side in and the odd size blocks faced out. Worked slick and once done I got busy and painted the outside with tar, along with covering the walls with sheets of plastic. Worked great for all the years we lived there and never had a leak. Once we back filled around the walls outside, one never seen the different sides of the old blocks and on the inside, well one would never know.

Well there you go, a bit about some old time things that once were, and how us older folks made use out of them.

Something
To Think About

Y ou know once in awhile I think folks should sit down and really think about certain things, like years ago versus today.

Here are a few examples: Places to get your milk.

Today, one just has to walk to the corner store.

Hmm, years ago I remember folks having milk delivered right to their door.

Bread and eggs, just go for a walk or drive to the supermarket.

Years ago we had them also delivered right to the door.

How about cuts, fractures and things, now a days we go to the doctor and wait in line for an hour or two, then pick up some cream of some sort at a drug store.

Years ago most husbands and wives knew how to look after a wound right at home themselves, fixed it up and was back in the field in less than ten minutes. Most every one had a couple Aloe Vera plants growing in or near their home somewhere, which they used for healing along with, Plantain and Comfrey.

Today folks have computers and things to keep notes or finding out information, not saying that is a bad thing, but years ago they weren't necessary as folks used the minds of their elders, along with their own. The old ribbon type writer or just a pencil was used to write things down and most every one carried a note pad in their shirt pocket or purse.

Automated bank machines is another. Back in my day we went to the bank and talked to a human being not a machine. We even had the bank manager over for supper once in awhile. Pretty hard to ask a machine over for a meal. Not to forget all the jobs that were lost when the machines were brought in.

Governments now a days, folks say we couldn't do without them.

Years ago before my time governments were just a word, no one ever seen them other than when it came time for wanting your vote.

Taxes, years ago the working man kept the money in their own pockets. Didn't look for help from the Powers That Be, didn't want it, wouldn't take it if they gave it to them.

Vacations, taking trips all over the world.

Years ago we took trips with a horse and buggy, a vacation would be out under a nice shade tree over-looking a meadow of wheat on a Sunday afternoon.

Tractors for the fields.

Years ago we used horses and didn't need to buy fuel, was unheard of, just grew hay instead.

Free trade, couple fine words, but that is all they ever were. In my books we didn't need to make them two words law in this country, we were doing quite well without them. I also feel that those two words, destroyed the folks that helped make this great country, the farmers. We had sort of free trade back when, the best kind, as we traded folks for what we didn't have, and not what we could grow or build ourselves. Worked good too and no money exchanged hands.

Entertainment, today we have movies, theaters, dances to go to, just too many to name, we spend thousands a year to go to these places.

Back in my day we had barn dances, no charge, dart games, no charge, horseshoes, no charge, and socials where folks met and had meals, no charge. Best of all, one could just go down town to the local feed mill, or barber shop, or anywhere on the main street, and sit and chat for hours about things. Can't get any better entertainment than that.

Phones now a days, cost the working man a thousand dollars a year almost, just to have one in the house, probably more if you figure in the Cell phone too.

Years ago didn't need any phones, enjoyed the peace of mind and if you wanted to talk to some one, you sent off a message with a passerby or dropped in for a visit.

Bathrooms of today, yes it's pretty nice not having to go out in the cold, but each year cost hundreds, if not thousands of dollars, just to relieve yourself each morning. On the farm we had an outhouse didn't cost us a cent, only work involved was digging a new hole once every couple years.

Stoves of today, seems to me it costs more to cook a roast of beef today than we pay for it.

Back in my day we cooked it in a wood stove, no charge, just the labor of bringing in the wood was all that was required. Also kept the house warm while cooking, no fuel bill every month.

Well I don't think it's necessary to mention anymore, as I am sure you get my meaning, which shows, that things of years past weren't all that bad.

Some say it was a hard life, I never looked at it like that for one minute. Todays world through my eyes is ten times more complicated, with every one running around working seven days a week, just to make ends meet, not having time to enjoy the important things in life.

I'd like to finish this book with these few words.

"I figure anyone that plants a garden or farms, believes in themselves, and your mistakes if recognized properly, brings forth nothing but rewards. When I was young, mornings were the best time of day, as the world has been born new and anything and everything, was possible."

I hope you have enjoyed the book as much as I have enjoyed writing it!

In Closing
I Would Like To Wish You Well